Cover photo by Rose Carbonell

©1998/2012 Steven Kenji Tazumi – all rights reserved
ISBN 978-1-300-36182-4

Chapters

This book is dedicated.

to my loving mother Terrie Tazumi,

my supportive father,

Tats Tazumi, who passed on April 21, 2000

and to my guardian angel,

Uncle Tosh Oye, who passed on

October 10, 2000

Forward

"If a man is judged by the number of friends he makes along the road to success then I am among the most blessed of men."

Many thanks to all my family, friends and business associates that have enlightened me along the way.

Healthfully yours,
Steven Kenji Tazumi
Proprietor,
Tazunmi Personal Training Service
www.tazunmi.com

About the Author

May 10, 1975 the author's coach, Mr. John Biaselli and the author. 1st Place Trophy, Olympic AAU Weight-lifting Nationals, Cleveland, Ohio.

December 28, 2012, Mr. Biaselli stops by to visit with the author at Tazunmi Personal Training Studio, Mullica Hill, NJ

Hi, my name is Steven Kenji Tazumi.

Who is Steve Tazumi? I have been in the health and fitness field for over 35 years. At age 13 I started weightlifting in an elementary school janitor's room in Bellmawr, New Jersey.

A volunteer coach was working with a small group of Olympic style weight lifters. This is where I had my first encounter with the sport of weightlifting.

In the beginning years as an Olympic weight lifter, I mastered correct form which, to this day, continues to be extremely helpful. I teach all my clients to use correct weight training form to help them maximize results and minimize potential injury.

This author started Olympic Weightlifting
At the age of 13 years old

Cleveland, Ohio National AAU Junior Olympics

In 1974, I placed first at the National AAU Junior Olympic Championships in the 114 lb. weight lifting class in the 14 - 15 years age group. In 1975 I took the gold in Olympic weightlifting at the junior nationals as a 114 pound class.

This author in standing next to his Local, National and International weightlifting trophies

Nineteen-eighty was the year that the United States did not go to the Olympic games in Moscow, Russia. I took third place at the Olympic trials at the Philadelphia Spectrum in the clean and jerk lift. I also represented the U.S. in two international meets against Canada, in one of which I won the gold medal for the USA.

Certificate of Participation

The United States Olympic Committee

is proud to recognize

STEVEN KENJI TAZUMI — 60K

as a candidate for the 1980 Olympic Team participating in

The Final Trials for the

Games of the XXII Olympiad

F. Don Miller
Executive Director

President

Sport ___ Weightlifting

Trials Site ___ Philadelphia, Pennsylvania

Trials Date ___ May 31 - June 1, 1980

Scoreboard at the Philadelphia Spectrum
1980 Olympic Trials

I am able to use all of my weightlifting experience and knowledge and apply it to every one of my clients. I took my hobby, and favorite sport, and first love, and turned it into a lucrative living. What a great life!

From 1984 to l991 I owned and operated a body building gym. I had two locations; one in Bellmawr, NJ, and the other in Runnemede, NJ.

Runnemede, NJ

Bellmawr, NJ

From 1992 through 1997 I committed my time to one of the largest health club chains in the United States, Bally's Total Fitness. I was a fitness instructor, personal trainer, Service Manager and General Manager. During that time, I also taught basic and advanced weightlifting at Camden County College, Blackwood, NJ.

I continued to teach weight lifting and served as a board member on the Advisory Committee for Health and Fitness Technology for Camden County College.

Granites Gym Power lifting Team

Weightlifting Teacher
Camden County College
Blackwood, NJ

I also served as Head Strength Coach for high school football teams in the Northeastern United States. My goal was to develop stronger offensive and defensive players for the teams.

What I have accomplished would not have been possible without the support and dedication of my early childhood weightlifting coach. Looking back, my coach Mr. John Biaselli was an individual dedicated to the sport of weight lifting, the art of body building, and the strength of power lifting. He has remarkable knowledge in the sport of iron, but never lifted a weight in his life. Mr. John Biaselli was able to produce several national and international weight lifting champions.

I greatly appreciate the impact Mr. Biaselli had on my life, personally and professionally. I am now able to share with my clients what I learned from Mr. Biaselli. To be a champion there is endless hours of work and dedication towards their sport or their specific goals, no matter what the weather or time of year. What people do not realize is the person behind the champion is the coach. "This is the person who also dedicates their life for you to achieve your specific goal. I would like to thank you, Mr. John Biaselli, for your dedication in the sport of iron and the development and growth of this particular individual.

Having over 200 trophies in Olympic weightlifting demonstrates solid experience; however it is important that you have additional certifications, such as:

1991 : United States Weightlifting Federation (USWF) Strength and Club Coach;

1992: Bally's Health and Fitness Certification Curriculum 1, 11, 111, Personal Trainer;

1993: Reebok Instructor Certification for Body Walking, 1, 11, 111, Advanced Personal Trainer.

2005 ISCA Kickboxing Certification

2007: AAAI Personal Fitness Trainer Certification

2007: NASM

I am AAU certified by the Amateur Athletic Union of the United States as an Amateur Body Building and Power Lifting Judge, and by the United States Weightlifting Federation as an Olympic Weightlifting Judge. I also volunteer my time as a bench press competition judge during the Special Olympics.

If you are going to be a personal trainer you should know about all three fields of weightlifting: Olympic Weightlifting, Powerlifting, and Body Building. Go to a competition to learn more about the organizations, and how the competitions work. Most importantly, be involved! .

The more knowledge, education and understanding you possess, the better you can serve your clients.

When I was in my 20's I competed in a Body Building Competition.

I am over 50 years of age now and I am competing in Drug Free Body Building Competitions.

What makes a great Personal Trainer?

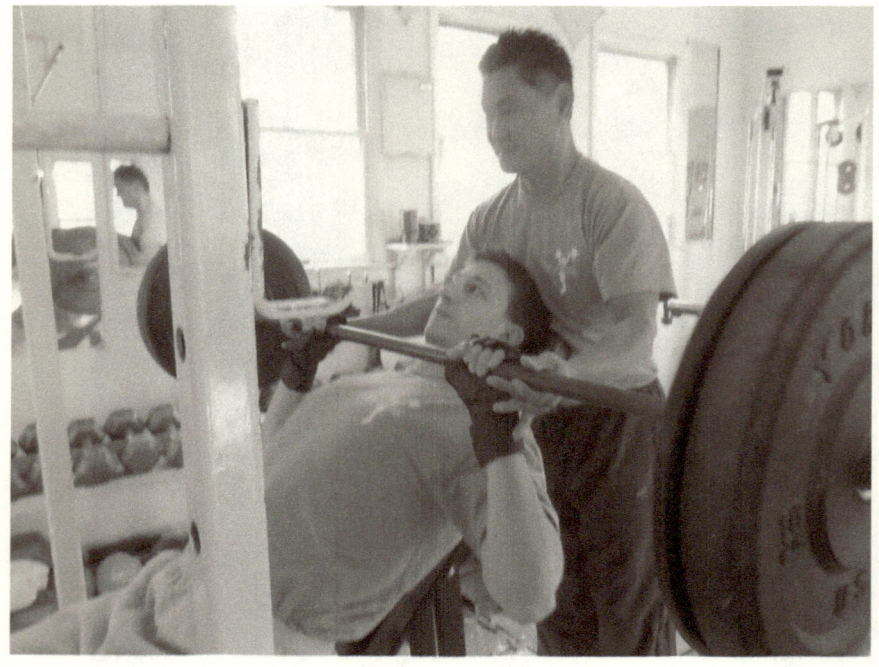

Author training longtime client, Josh Kanstantinos

Welcome to the most rewarding occupation in the world, Personal Training! This occupation is gratifying in so many ways. Best of all you control your destiny and provide the guidance your clients need to achieve their goals.

Think of personal training as a journey. Along the way, you learn to teach, motivate, enhance self esteem, and create new ideas that will help someone to achieve their personal goals. You develop a successful plan for tracking and monitoring your client's progress, to help them achieve the results they truly desire. I love this business because I am helping all of my clients in a way that is custom-tailored to their personal needs. Each person's journey is a new adventure with a new story line.

In the year 2000 I met my identical twin brother, Tom Patterson, for the first time since we were infants. Through all the meeting and the getting to know each other, the interviews and the discussions, the one thing that stood out in my mind was that we both had a natural born desire for the physical fitness field. We were raised in different environments.

Tom grew up in Liberal, Kansas in a rural Christian home. I was raised in Bellmawr, New Jersey in a suburban Buddhist home. Tom was a power lifter who had owned his own commercial gym, called Ultra Fitness Spa and I was an Olympic Weightlifter and owned two commercial body building gyms, Granites Gym I and II. The desire to be into physical fitness came naturally to us. So I would say that the first thing a great personal trainer has is a natural desire to work in the physical fitness field.

To be an effective as a personal trainer you have to be outgoing. If you are a shy person or you are introverted you would have to over these obstacles. First, practice training one on one with a family member, then with a friend, then a client. If you have trouble dealing on a one on one basis you can try teaching small groups in exercise. This will allow you to practice giving physical fitness information to people until you are comfortable with your knowledge and ability and can better work one on one.

You must have a strong personality without being overbearing. Your demeanor must be such that people want to follow your lead, they must feel comfortable taking instruction from you but not intimidated by you.

Another trait you must have is to be able to communicate well whether one on one or with groups. If you have trouble communicating or expressing yourself in public, a way you can overcome this is by taking public speaking courses.

The first three minutes meeting someone you will know if you like them or if they like you. Being able to recognize how they feel about you will help you in establishing a good relationship. When you sit down with a potential client on their initial orientation, they will tell you their story. From the very beginning you need to be empathetic to them. You must be able to recognize what they are feeling because this will set the tone of the meeting and their sessions. Keep in mind everyone is totally different and each person has their own situation and feelings towards them. Every journey is unique.

You must be goal oriented. This is true with your clients and also in your business and personal life. You have to be able to set goals, short term and long term term. This characteristic is so important. If you are not goal oriented, how can you help anyone else out? I am constantly reviewing and evaluating my goals in my life, with my clients and my business 24/7.

You must practice what you preach. I have seen so many personal trainers in my lifetime that were fat and overweight or talking to their clients about how much they party all night long. I have also seen trainers smoking cigarettes and then training a client with the stench of cigarettes on their breath. We will talk about this more in further in the book.

Last, but not least, the most important, number one thing is **PASSION!** You must love what you do and your true heart must be into it. If you are happy with what you do, your client will respond to that, if not, the client will see right through you. Even if this is a 10:00 pm last session after a thirteen hour day, you must have as much enthusiasm and spirit as with your first client of the day. I love going to work every single day of the week and would not have it any other way. The winners in life have one common denominator, and that is TRUE PASSION in what they do.

Who needs a personal trainer?

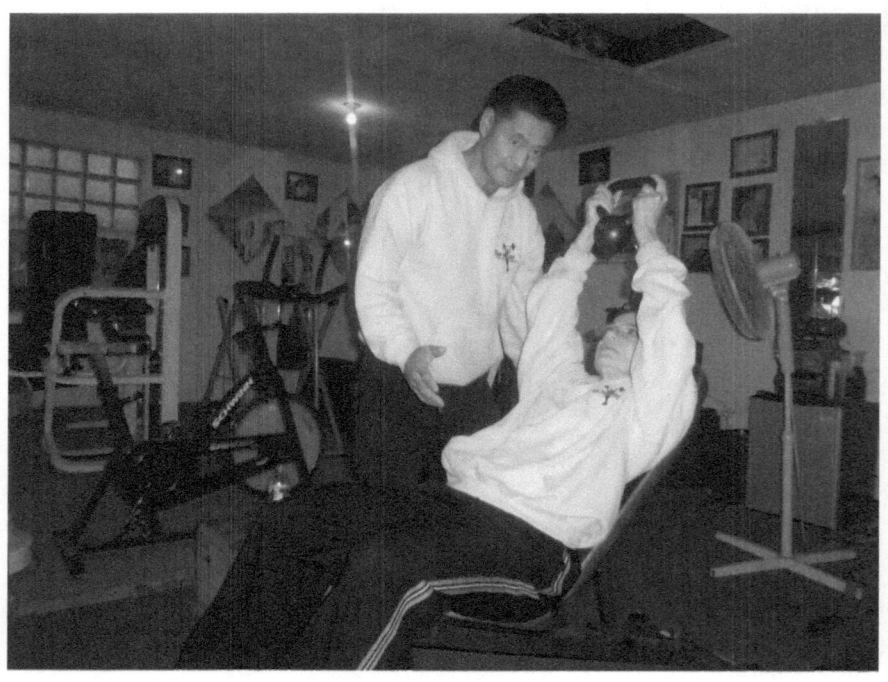

Personal Trainer Rose Carbonell, being trained by Steven Tazumi, the author, both of Tazunmi Personal Training Service.

Remember, everyone needs a personal trainer. Even Personal trainers need Personal Trainers.

What do I mean by this? I have seen so many Personal Trainers and teachers who look like they should be the client and not the teacher or coach. They are out of shape, overweight and have no idea what fitness is all about (except what they might have read in a textbook while eating fattening snacks in front of the television). I have also seen trainers smoking cigarettes.

Practice what you preach!

As a Personal Trainer, you have an image to project to the public! Would you buy a health club membership from a person that is overweight and smoking a cigar and drinking a beer in front of you? I would not! That's why Personal Trainers need other Personal Trainers to help them develop and refine their own personal goals. For example your Personal Trainer may want to go into a body building con- test, and would like your advice on how to pose effectively.
They value your unbiased opinion and thorough under- standing of body building competitions. In this case, another Personal Trainer may be one of your valued assets.

There are many other people who can also benefit from your services. An up and coming clientele base is senior citizens. You have to realize that people are living longer. The lifestyle senior citizens have chosen is much more active.
For example, the majority of senior citizens in the state of Florida lead a very productive and happy life. It is not uncommon to see a 70-90 year old senior citizen playing golf or tennis, or even in the gym pumping iron. In the exclusive San Diego California community of La Jolla, senior citizens are up early to fast walk, jog or run. They are taking to the beautiful blue Pacific Ocean for

recreational and competitive swimming. Some swimmers exceed one mile. It's become a New Years Day tradition that many prepare for all year long. Your role as Personal Trainer must be to realize how important it is to serve this large population of senior citizens ethically and professionally.

Personal Trainers are also needed in the medical field. For example, after rehabilitation following an accident or illness, a physician may advise a patient to work one-on-one with a Personal Trainer for continued or advanced rehabilitation. Clients may also contact you at critical points in their life. For example, when they recognize they need help, or when they learn from their doctor it is time to get on a regular exercise program (or they could end up six feet under!)

In any case you should always consult your client's physicians before setting up an exercise program for them.
Follow their physician's advice closely, and keep in touch with their physician. Do not attempt to be a hero! Health insurance plans are also picking up some of the costs of a personal trainer, so consult your insurance carrier.

Many people ask when the best age to start lifting weights is. The best age to start lifting weights is at the age of 11 and over. The bones and muscles are better able to handle weights and resistance training. This is a great time to have your child involved in a weight training program. Weight training will put your child on a path to learning how to take care of their bodies, and help to improve diet and sleep patterns. It may also deter them from negative influences in today's world like drinking and drugs.

Start teenagers in a very slow and easy program. The hardest part about working with teenagers is their attention span; it is very short and interest levels are usually lower.

The idea that results are quick and simple is farthest from the truth. Take your time with children. They can become very trying at times but they are also very enjoyable, active and most of all rewarding to work with!

How about the rich and famous? This is one of the toughest groups to work with, but also the most rewarding. This clientele is very demanding in all ways and fashions. These members are very goal oriented and on a very tight time schedule; their time is money!

In their eyes, time spent with you is money lost.

They do not understand the value of a healthy body and how it in turn creates a healthy mind that can lead to a more productive life and income. They want results yesterday and cannot comprehend how hard it is to achieve their personal goals. You have to work out with them on their time schedule, not yours. Remember, in their minds, you are replaceable.

They are very picky and want results immediately. Your job is to provide them with a wide variety of exercises to keep the program fresh, new and ever changing. They do not like the same exercise day in and day out. You have to be very creative!

This is a challenge for you. The best thing about working with the rich and famous is that if he or she likes you and your training style, you will be the hit of the town and your business will skyrocket!

There is another client group similar to the rich and famous. However, they have realistic expectations and attitudes about physical fitness: athletes and models. This clientele's entire future depends on their physical appearance and/or physical performance. They are also very goal oriented. They want results yesterday, they are very demanding, and yes, their time is also money. However, they do realize the advantage of physical fitness because it is their primary source of income!

The major difference between the rich and famous and your athlete and model is that the athlete and model will work out extremely hard, and will do whatever it takes to look great or perform their very best! This may even include their desire for steroid usage, which I am totally against. Your role as a Personal Trainer is to clearly explain the dangers of anabolic steroids to your athlete and model clients. It is your ethical and professional obligation to your clients.

Where to Personal Train

Using nature – An obstacle course uses a large variety of skills while enjoying nature.

When deciding on the best location to train clients, Personal Trainers have many options from which to choose. I feel that Mother Nature gave us a beautiful planet to work out in so why not just use it! Most of us work an eight to ten hour day, and are seldom exposed to sunshine, except possibly through a window if you are lucky enough to have one in your office or workplace.

I love to take my clients for walks in the park or along a safe roadside. This is a great time to really get to know your clients and talk about their day. In additions it gives them a chance to see the outside world, unwind and relax. This is also very enjoyable for both of you. The walk doesn't have to be at a slow pace. You can test your client's abilities by doing wind sprints from one telephone pole (or tree) to another, or you can go in your car and measure out a mile and time your clients. You can cross train with sprinting, jogging, and then walking. You can also set up an outside obstacle course. Using nature as your personal training grounds can be fun and exciting, but remember to check the weather forecast in advance, since weather conditions may not always be predictable. Enjoy nature. It's a great way to start a work-out!

Another great place to train or work out with your client is in their house. This is great for your client, but can be very trying for the Personal Trainer. You must incorporate the travel time between locations and give yourself adequate time in case of traffic or weather delays. These time considerations should be figured in when you give your client an hourly price.

Be fair with your price, but remember, time is money. If you have to travel half an hour to a location you must double it to account for the return trip. Add your service cost.

Working out of a client's house can also be hard if the client does not have the proper equipment to help them achieve their goals.

The equipment may be outdated, too advanced, too difficult to use, or may not have been properly maintained.

Often you as the trainer will need to bring your workout equipment, music, and mats to your client's home. This can turn into a long day when you are lifting more weights than your clients! Another problem with working out of some- one's house is that you are on "their turf." What do I mean by this? You get to your client's house and you are ready to train them but the client has a family problem to resolve.

Or, your client is on a business call that may take another 10-15 minutes; their children require attention or have emergency needs (i.e., wet diapers, feeding time, setting up the baby-sitter or TV time, etc.)

This all takes time and most important, you cannot say too much about these instant emergencies, or you will lose a client. Remember, this is their turf, not yours. As a personal trainer you will need to be insured. Personally, I never liked working out at my client's house because you may accidentally break their equipment or personal belongings.

Also, in this day and age you must be aware of sexual advances and sexual harassment.

I never liked the idea of a closed door at someone's house during personal training. You may be asking for trouble!

Another location is a commercial gym. This is a great location to establish your client base. You know that you have a captive audience. Be sure, though, that you get approval from the gym management.

When it comes to physical fitness, there are all different types of people with own personal agenda, i.e. body- builders, business executives, and laborers. Each group values physical conditioning but their personal goals are quite different from one another.

Remember, this is business and I mean big business. You as a personal trainer must show your credentials, your insurance, and also pay a rental fee for using the gym. This fee can be established by the managing team for your gym or health club.

In smaller bodybuilding gyms you can work out a percent- age fee for using the gym, for example, a 50/50 split, 75/25 split, or a set fee for every session. Be creative. You will be surprised at what type of arrangements can be worked out.
You are an asset to your gym or health club, and it can be a win-win relationship.

In my opinion, your house or studio is a preferable place to train your clients. The overhead is established by your rent or mortgage. You are in an environment that you control.
You are on your turf and not someone else's. You have full control of the type of equipment required to train your clients. If you accidentally break any personal belongings it is yours! If you break any equipment it is yours!

My studio is located away from my house. This keeps my business separate from my daily living. My studio has 10 windows and no curtains or shades. Anyone can look in at any time and see my client and me working out. The door is always open. This keeps the opposite sex much more comfortable than in a studio that is totally closed, and prevents any type of sexual advances, or sexual harassment.

The Business Plan:
Your Personal and
Professional Goals

THE MIRROR
Every day you wake up and look at yourself in the mirror The mirror is a reflection of what the world thinks and sees of you. Are you happy with what you see?

In my business flyer I wrote of a concept which I called "The Mirror." Every day you wake up and look at yourself in the mirror. The mirror is a reflection of what the world thinks of you and how you are seen. Are you happy with what you see?

The very first personal goal is to look at yourself. I have seen so many personal trainers, gym teachers, and gym owners who look like they should be the client, and not the instructor. Remember, teach what you preach!

You must begin a workout program if you are not currently working out. If you are not watching your diet, you will look in your mirror and see someone out of shape and fat. How are you ever going to persuade someone to work out if you don't do it yourself Today is the day to start working out!

Folks, I have a very big problem with this! I'm not saying you have to be a body builder; however, I am saying you have to be in shape. When was the last time you ran? When was the last time you lifted the iron? If you do not like to do any physical exercise yourself you may have to think twice about becoming a Personal Trainer.

This may sound harsh but I see so many people in this field that should be in another career.

I have seen health club workers smoking cigarettes, and/or drinking at their jobs. If you are going to teach health and fitness you must set an example. You are your greatest selling tool! You are the biggest and most convincing billboard!

Now the real work begins. First, a mental exercise. Before setting up your goals, find a location that is quiet and very relaxing and start asking yourself a number of critical questions. These questions may not be answered right away, and that is OK.

This exercise is just to make you think about yourself, a self-assessment. Remember you are the personal trainer and your ideas and personal values will also come out while working together with your clients. Ready? Let's begin!

Here are some questions you should ask yourself:

- Do I want to gain weight? How much? By what date?
- Do I want to lose weight? How much? By what date?
- Do I want to go into a body building contest, or a fitness contest? By what date?
- Do I want to increase my poundage in a certain exercise? How much? By what date?
- What is my plan of action; what do I want to do?
- How many inches do I want to gain, or reduce? By what date?
- Do I have to lower my blood pressure? How much? By what date?
- Do I have to bring down my cholesterol? How much? By what date?

Get a sheet of paper and pencil and write down your responses to each question above.

Let's continue. Now that you have your health and physical goals writ- ten down, let's work on your family goals. What do I mean by this? We are often on the run and sometimes forget one of the most important parts of our personal world. This is the circle of our family. You are part of the circle and you define yourself within the context of this circle.

Let's ask ourselves some questions:

- Do I want to get closer to my mother?
- Do I want to get closer to my father?
- Do I want to get closer to my brother?
- Do I want to get closer to my sister?
- Do I want to see my grandmother, or grandfather more often?
- Do I want to spend more time with the entire family; get to know my family roots?
- Do I want to spend more quality time with my spouse and children?
- Do I want to spend more time with my uncles or aunts?

If your answer to these questions is "yes" then you need to find the means of spending more time with your family. For example, take your mother to lunch. By when? Next Monday afternoon. You may know of someone that has passed away. Go to their gravesite, spend time alone there and let them know that they are still a big part of your life, and always will be! No matter how busy my schedule gets, I always put aside a time for my mother every week. I put it on my work calendar so members know that a certain time is dedicated to my mother.

Let's talk about friends and peer groups. Making friends is a goal many of us set. You may not think so, but birds of a feather do flock together. You don't often find a millionaire or high power executive hanging around with the alcoholic on skid row. The rich and famous prefer to socialize with multi-million dollar friends.

Let's ask ourselves a few more questions:

- Do you want to use Facebook, Twitter, LinkedIn, etc.
- Do I want to meet that special person? What type? Are their interests the same as yours?
- Do I want to spend more time with my friends?
- Are your friends helping you with your goals or are they destroying your goals? For example, if you are training for a body

building contest are your friends helping you by making sure you are eating the right foods and getting enough sleep? Or, are your friends asking you to go out to night clubs, staying out all hours of the night drinking alcoholic beverages and eating fatty foods at fast food restaurants (they are sabotaging your goal). I see this with couples sabotaging each other.

- Do I want to go out? Do I want go by myself or with others? Where do I want to go? Does it matter if I go alone?
- Do I want to go out to the clubs? What type? Why?
- Do I have a plan? (i.e.) If I drink too much is there someone there to drive me home?

Write down your goals and answers. And be honest with yourself.

Now let's talk about spiritual goals. This is one of three subjects we do not often discuss. My mother would always tell me not to discuss religion, politics, or sex in social settings because everyone has their own value system.

Let us ask ourselves some questions:

- Do I want to go to church? What type of church?
- Do I want to go to church more often? How many times more?
- Do I only go to church or pray when something is wrong in my personal or family life?
- How can I change this?
- Would I like to read more about religion?
- What type of books?
- I am not religious at all, but I need some quiet time. Where would I like to spend my quiet time? How will I spend my quiet time?

Write down your spiritual feelings. Set a specific time to accomplish these goals. Don't hesitate, just do it!

Let's talk about your state of mind. Have you ever seen someone that is always in a very bad mood or always negative? It does not matter when you see this person. Morning, noon and night they are always complaining about how the world isn't right! And how society did them wrong, or because of their parents they are like this today!

It is very tough to be around these people because they always bring you down with their conversations. On the other hand have you ever seen someone who is always very positive, and a joy to be around? They're always happy, or is there more to this?

Our state of mind is under our own control. You have to retrain yourself to think and be positive. There are many books, tapes and videos on the subject of positive thinking.

These books, tapes and videos are enjoyable, educational and will really get you thinking. This is good because today's society steals people's humanity. People are turned into machines and machines have no personality! You have two choices; negative or positive. You make the choice, and remember you ALONE are responsible for your actions. No one else!

Some more questions to ask yourself:

• Would I like to be a more positive person? How am I going to do this?
• Do I want to concentrate better? How am I going to accomplish this?
• Do I want to change my feelings toward my spouse to improve our marriage?
• How can I do this? What is my plan?
• Do I want to stop smoking? What is my plan? What is the date I want to stop?
• Do I want to stop drinking? What is my plan? By what date?

The last goal is a combination of finances, education, and business planning. All of these are interconnected. Let's look at the entire picture.

You want to be a personal trainer. You first have to look at yourself. What type of image do you want to project? With what type of client do you want to work? Is there a certain client you do not want to work with? Where do you want to train someone? Is there a demand for your service in this area? Have you looked at the demographics in your area? Have you investigated your competition?

These questions must be answered honestly. Take your time, and think these answers through! These are the foundations for your company. These basic ideas will be your building blocks for developing your personal training business. You are on your way to setting up your business plan and goals.

Teaching is essential for personal trainers. I taught college for over ten years, and was involved on an advisory committee for health and fitness technology for the college.

This experience not only keeps me fresh, and up-to-date with all of the new health developments in our field, but also keeps me in-tune with the next generation of students that want to become personal trainers.

It helps me to understand their needs, feelings and individual concerns in today's world, since the world of fitness is always changing.

Certifications are very important as part of your continuing education. You must be aware of how and where to attain these certifications.

Now, ask yourself some personal questions:

- Do I want to go to a two year college? A four year college? Get my masters or doctorate?
- Do I want to get a personal training certification?
- Do I want to attend workshops?
- Is education important in my personal training business?
- Is my staff well educated?
- What will I do to continue my staff's education? For example, there are seminars, in-service meetings, continuing education and/or certifications.

You now have an idea of your business image, and have determined your educational values as they relate to your business.

Now lets talk about financial goals. You have to set up goals even when it relates to money or buying any type of product or equipment. For example, I had a Honda that I drove over one hundred thousand miles. I loved that car! The next car I would buy would be a step above, an Acura. I knew I wanted a bright red car, with stick shift and a sun roof. I called all the car dealers in the tri-state area, and I finally found the best price for the car. I felt great because I bought the car I wanted! The sales person could not believe that I wanted to buy this car without a test drive! I knew that I had a Honda that was very good to me. Why wouldn't an Acura be the same or better? I know many people walk into a sales situation and end up buying something they didn't intentionally come in to buy. If you want to buy a blue car, make sure you get that blue car. If you don't you will never be totally happy with your decision.

Remember, this is your car, not the salesperson's. You, and not the salesperson, will have to live with your decision! What I am saying is that all your financial decisions are made by making up your own mind and setting concrete goals. This is how you will be happy with all the financial decisions you make in your lifetime! Know exactly what you want!

Everyone wants to make money. This is why you bought this book! Again, you must ask yourself some very important questions. Every day you should be re-evaluating your goals; this keeps you fresh!

- Do I want a lot of money?
- What do you consider to be a lot of money?
- How much money? By when?
- What is my plan?
- How long will it take to make my money?
- Can I run my business alone? Do I need partners?
- Will I run my business as a corporation?
- Will I need financial backing?
- Where will I go to get additional funds?

All of these questions are very important. It will require some thought to come up with all the answers. It may take a year or two so don't rush yourself. Be patient and answer all questions honestly.

In your business plan, you now have an idea of your company profile. For example, your company image, the level of education you want to achieve or you want your staff to achieve, how much money you would like to make, and what type of structure you would like to have in your own personal training company. Today companies call it a mission statement.

But your work is not complete just because of these inner thoughts you have written down. The next step is to take this paper and put it aside for approximately one to three months. Then, take it out again, and go to a quiet place and re-evaluate these goals again.

See if your ideas and goals have changed. There is a good chance that they have.

The Formula for Success - 5 Simple Steps!

1. Plan for Success

Let's look at the formula for success which applies to any goal that you desire, no matter what it may be: starting your own personal training business, business goals, financial goals, physical goals social goals, educational goals, mental goals, family goals, and spiritual goals. Plan your work and work your plan.

2. Set Goals

For example, my long term goal is that I would like to have 50 clients; my short term goal is I would like to have 5 clients. When you secure your first five clients reward your- self. Take yourself out to dinner; buy yourself a new sweat- suit or a new piece of equipment. Reward yourself because guess what? It's working and you are doing a great job. You
are on your way!

When you secure your next five clients, again reward your- self, then re-evaluate your original long term goal; i.e., I would like to get 50 clients. Once you have achieved this goal again buy yourself a new car, take a cruise, and take your staff out to dinner. This is also time to reflect on your success and re-evaluate your new goals again. Let all of your friends and family know about your goals. They will support you and help you. You should evaluate your goals four times a year or when the seasons change.

Give yourself a deadline. You can always change this date, but it gives you a time frame in which to accomplish your goals. Half the fun in accomplishing your goal is your journey. Just don't quit, keep on trucking! The turtle won the race.

3. Think Positive!

No one ever accomplished a goal by thinking negatively! Remember you have a choice when you wake up every day of your life: think negative, or think positive. Positive people get what they want out of their life, and they are a pleasure to be around. Is the glass half full or half empty. I say half full, always.

4. Visualize Your Success

If you bought this book you are trying to better yourself and I congratulate you!! If there is someone you admire, someone you see as a role model, you should first visualize your- self being that person. For example, if you want to be a personal trainer, go to a personal trainer and talk to them about the positives and negatives about the business. You may even have to pay for a consultation with a trainer. This would be worth a lot of knowledge and money for you. The more knowledge you have the better off you will be.

This time is very valuable. You may find out that personal training is what you want. You may also find out that personal training is not what you thought it to be. You must go back and re-evaluate what you would like to be, and repeat the process again.

5. Work Your Plan

Your assignment once you come up with a plan - WORK IT! Life is a plan, and you determine your destiny. So just do it! I know so many people who plan to do so many things when they retire, like travel the world, or play golf everyday. But guess what? They don't do anything but dream! You have to follow through with your personal goals. Could have and should have won't work. If you follow this plan you will be at the top of your field, no matter what it may be. The most rewarding part of your journey is that this book is for you. I wish you the best of luck in achieving your goals no matter what they are. This book can be utilized in every job field or situation and aspect of life not only personal training. All day long we are selling ourselves no matter what the product is. So tell a friend and enjoy this journey with me.

Selling Yourself and Your Business

Selling your name and selling your products. . . .

The first advertisement is you. **You are a walking billboard.** If you look as if you are the one who needs a personal trainer you have a very big problem! You and your looks are the best form of advertisement. Once again you must ask yourself:

- What do you wear to the gym?
- What do you wear during work?
- What do you wear during your leisure time, and social events?

The correct answer is your uniform. Every shirt I wear in public has the name of my business on it. Every sweatsuit I wear has my business logo. All of my jackets have my business logo, phone number and website. You are a personal trainer and you must show the world who you are. Where should you advertise? The answer is simple. When you are driving in your car use magnetic signs to advertise your business, or get your car or truck painted. This of course will depend on state regulations regarding registration of a commercial vehicle.

At your home or studio business location have a logo that shows that you are a personal trainer. Post a sign with your business name. Again, check with your state or local laws before doing this. You may need to acquire a permit.

Flyers are a very effective method of advertising. You must show your image, and put it on your flyer. You may have to give out thousands of flyers before you get any response, but the one response will pay for the cost of your flyers. In your flyer have something that catches the eye. For example:

- Are you tired of being overweight?
- Are you tired of being out of breath and out of shape?
- Are you tired of everyday stress with no relief or physical activity?
- Are you a number at your gym and not a name?

- Are you tired of no results?
- Are you tired of waiting for equipment?
- Are you promised the world and getting nothing.

The introductory part of your flyer should tell a story about you-who you are, your background, certifications, education, achievements in physical fitness.

The body of your flyer should be about the features and benefits of your company. For example:

Tazunmi Personal Training Service offers fitness testing, nutrition assistance, a private fitness studio, package programs, Olympic lifting, power lifting, body building, sports and strength team training, and custom programs for senior citizens.

You can use this format in print, radio, TV and Internet advertising. Newspaper, magazine and other print advertisement prices are determined by the size and positioning of your ad. You also have Facebook, Twitter, LinkedIn, etc.

You do not have enough time to tell an entire story about yourself. The general public only wants to know the price and is often unaware of services, (i.e.) Get your own personal trainer for only $24.99, or, for $24.99 you can be treated like a Hollywood Star and have your own personal trainer or, you can be the best for only $24.99 and have your own personal trainer. Notice how I used the price in the end, beginning, and middle of each ad.

Be creative. This is your business and there are no set rules-the sky is the limit!

TV shows and newspaper articles are excellent opportunities to show off your business. Just as you did with flyers, you must gain audience attention. Tell a story about you! And then give them your features and benefits and how you can be contacted.

Look your very best, it may be your only shot. Make sure to show your company logo, be well groomed, and by all means, be prepared! TV shows can really put you on the map.

Personal referrals are the oldest and best form of advertising. Client testimonials will be the foundation of your business. If your clients are happy with your service they will tell 10 people. If they are not happy with your service they will tell 100 people. Which would you prefer?

The buddy referral system is the best system, clients telling other clients. There isn't a better system out there! Encourage them to advertise your company. Give them your company tee shirt, your company gym bags, your company towels, your company watches. Watch what happens. Your giveaways and gifts are you, and it is a reflection on your company. Do it right or don't do it at all. You are sending a message with your giveaways and gifts. 'They should always be positive. **Don't be cheap**! Remember, this is your company image!

Client/Member Orientations

The author showing Rose Finocchiaro his opening presentation.

From your business goals you now have a business plan, as well as a personal image of your company. Now with the right advertising, you will have your first client knocking at your door. Let the journey begin. Get excited! I sure am!

First Impressions

What do I do now? In the first 60 seconds a person has made up his or her unconscious mind; they've decided whether or not they will use your service. It's extremely important that your personal appearance be proper. What do I mean by this? Dress in your company sweatsuit or uniform. If you are a male, you should be clean-shaven, hair well groomed shirt tucked into your pants or sweat pants.
Use very little cologne if any; the persons that you are going to interview may have allergies. Your sneakers should be new or new looking. They should be part of your uniform and not be used outside. Women should wear little makeup, and have hair well groomed, nails done. Again use very little perfume if any. Sneakers should be new, or new looking, and be part of your uniform. They are not to be used out- side. You should wear athletic clothes during the client inter- view. Remember, you are not in a fashion show or a model. Both males and females should brush their teeth or use mouth wash. This is important because you will be very close to your client during the interview and work-out. Your office should be very business-like. For example, pictures and articles about you or your clients, your personal fitness trophies and certifications, and college degrees should be visible to your client.

Make your office professional and comfortable for your client. If you are going to a gym see if you can find a quiet area or room to talk to your prospective client. If you are going to someone's house, also find a quiet area or room to talk. If possible, do not interview your client with children present, or TV or radio on.

Buy yourself a durable 3 ring binder or book. This will be your presentation book. This book will sell you and your services. This is great to use when you are traveling to different locations.

This is how it works. Once you have someone interested in your services you must present yourself in a very professional manner. This book will help you do just that. You can put anything you want in this book, but remember, this book is to sell you and your services. Make sure each page of this book is laminated. Your presentation book must tell a short and sweet story about you and your services, and the features of your business.

Let's get started. Put your own personal health and fitness resume together. Place it into your book. Include pictures of you in competition: bodybuilding meets, aerobic competition, marathon running meets, competitions, MMA meets, cross fitness training. Use a recent picture, as well as a picture from your past (for example you weighing 300 pounds and now weighing 125 pounds). Anything that puts you into the limelight and increases your exposure will increase your business.

Include newspaper articles of you, your business, and your clients' before-and-after shots. But first, you must get per- mission to use your clients' pictures for this purpose. You should use client testimonials that acknowledge your success in working with them, their pictures, and any letters thanking you for your services in the past or present.
Include any diagram or picture that shows health or personal training, i.e. how to get your body in shape and proper nutrition. Include pictures showing how to improve your appearance, tone your body, and reduce heart attacks. Show
a picture of average people using a personal trainer, not only stars. Take pictures of your family. Tell your prospective clients that you work out because you want to enjoy your children, and see them grow to a ripe old age. Remind them that they can too! Remember

the old adage; a picture says a thousand words. In my office it looks like a museum with before and after pictures. People love to see success stories

At the end of your presentation book you should have the features of your business and also your price structure. I have a gold, silver and bronze program. Here is how it works. You now have your presentation book; this book is all about you and your company and also an information book on the benefits of health and fitness.

What about the prospective client? What I do is use both the presentation book and the personal interview together. I will use the presentation book in the beginning to introduce myself and my business, and then go to a personal interview with my client. I go back to the presentation book for additional reinforcement during the personal interview. "Mr.
Jones I see you have a history of heart disease. Let me show you a picture of how working out can help decrease your potential for heart disease". Then go to your presentation book. I will go back and forth depending on when I need it.
Remember, at the end of the interview go back to the presentation book and then discuss your membership price structure.

Let's talk about a personal interview. This is a very important feature in your orientation. Your clients want to know about you, but they are there for themselves. This is why they are coming to you! *HINT: A great icebreaker is to talk about what a client is wearing, for example if he/she is wearing a hat, t-shirt or sweats with a name or logo, such as a Philadelphia Phillies hat, you know they like the Phillies and you can start the conversation talking about them. People wear clothing to show what they enjoy or like. It is very important to know about current events and also what's going on in the sports world. A lot of people wear sports team's logos. You should know about each team. This puts you in a very positive light with your prospective member and will open up doors of communication.

An interview is a series of questions that are directed to your prospective clients to help you make a judgment on their physical conditioning and fitness level. Ask your clients questions and then listen! I know so many people who don't let the member say or finish what they would like to express. The personal trainer is trying to be the expert and overstepping their bounds by not letting the prospective member speak their mind. You have already lost your customer if you don't let them talk! <u>Shut up and listen!</u>

Here are sample questions you may want to ask during your personal interview. Make up your own questions. These questions will provide you with a great foundation and orientation. Good luck.

General Information

- Their name, address, city, state and zip code?
- Their home phone number? Their cell phone number?
- Their Email address, website, Facebook, LinkedIn and twitter
- Their place of work?
- Their work phone number?
- Status: married, single, divorced?
- Date of birth?
- Contact person in case of emergency?
- Contact person's phone number?
- Their doctors name, phone number?
- Have they ever worked out before?

Exercise & Recreational Activity Interview

- When was the last time they worked out?
- Where did they work out?

- What type of equipment do they have?
- What is their favorite exercise?
- What is their least favorite exercise?
- Do they want to reduce?
- Do they want to gain?
- Do they want to build?
- In what shape do they want to be by next year?
- How many days a week would they like to work out?
- Do they have any physical problems?
- Do they want to change their physical appearance?
- What type of music do they enjoy?
- Is music a big part in their work-out?
- Do they consider bodybuilding to be a sport, a job, art, enjoyment or relaxation?
- Do they plan on making money in bodybuilding?
- Do they expect to be sponsored?
- Do they mind traveling?
- Do they do any cardiovascular exercise?
- What type of cardiovascular exercises do they do?
- Do they play any sports?
- What is their favorite sport?
- What is their least favorite sport?
- What do they think about steroids?
- What do they think about health foods?
- What do they think about amino acids?
- How is their daily diet?
- How did they get involved in weight training?
- How many hours do they want to work out?
- What do they expect from their instructor?
- How do they feel about home work?
- What do they think about videos, DVD's and Blueray?
- Is their spouse or boyfriend/girlfriend supportive?
- What time do they like to work out?
- Would they like the trainer to work out with them?
- How did they hear about our service?

Health History

- Do they have any back problems?
- Do they have any leg problems?
- Do they have any bicep problems?
- Do they have any tricep problems?
- Do they have any deltoid (shoulder) problems, front, side, rear?
- Do they have any trapezius problems?
- Do they have any latissimus dorsi problems?
- Do they have any pectorals major or minor problems?
- Do they have any stomach problems?
- Do they have any hip problems?
- Do they have any calf problems?
- Do they have any gluteus maximum problems?
- Do they have any forearm problems?
- Do they have any wrist problems?
- Do they have problems holding/gripping anything?
- Do they smoke? How much?
- Do they drink? How much do they drink?
- Do they take any drugs? What type?
- Do they take any medication? What for? What type?
- Do they have any allergies?
- Do they have a any heart problems?
- Do they have a family history of heart problems?
- Do they have high or low blood pressure?
- Do they have a family history of high or low blood pressure?
- Do they know if they have high or low cholesterol?
- Do they have any family history of high or low blood cholesterol?
- Are they on any type of diet at this time?
- Do they have diabetes?
- Do they have any family history of diabetes?
- Do they have asthma?
- Are their any other medical problems I should be aware of?

- When was their last doctor's visit? Their doctor's name/phone number?
- Does their doctor know that they are going to begin an exercise program?
- Are there any special instructions I should get from your doctor?
- Do you have a medical release to start an exercise program?

Closing the Sale

If you leave one door open you will lose the sale.

After your interview you can now go into your price presentation. This is what it is all about. Don't let any one fool you! If you think that sales is not a part of the job you are mistaken. If you are the type of person who thinks that you only want to train somebody, but don't want to sell anyone, personal training may not be for you. Remember, to train someone you have to sell someone on you, your abilities and your business!! You are selling an abstract picture of what the client would like to be.

This can be very hard at times. Like it or not, sales is a part of our every day life. You may say you don't want to be in sales, or you hate to sell, or you'd rather be in the service end of a company, rather than the sales end, but if you stop to think about it, you will realize that you are selling every- day of your life. Why do I say this? Let's talk about dating.
Or should I say selling? When you go out on your dates, you are on your best behavior. You are dressed to kill, you are very polite, and you are making sure that every sentence makes sense, you are opening doors, giving flowers making dinners, giving gifts. You are selling to your date.

Let's talk about shopping. When you go shopping you know that someone is trying to sell you, don't you? You are also selling yourself. Big Sale! 50 percent off this winter jacket. You know the store is trying to sell you this jacket. You are debating, either consciously or unconsciously whether you would like to buy this winter jacket. You are trying to sell yourself on this nice, warm attractive white jacket. The next day you may go back to the store, or go to another store to compare prices or jackets, or talk to a salesperson about this warm, beautiful feathered, white jacket. The sales person is trying to sell you on a special zipper feature of this nice warm, feathered white zippered jacket.

You ask the salesperson, "Does this jacket have a hood?" And the sales person replies, "do you need a hood?" "Yes" you say. "I need a hood for skiing." "If I can get you the same jacket with a hood, for the same price, would you purchase this jacket today?" "Yes!"

The salesperson then brings out a nice warm, feathered, hooded white jacket. The sales person was able to meet your needs and personal desire. And you can justify the sale because you had input on exactly what you wanted, a hood- ed jacket. It is a sales situation that happens every day.

You may debate about having a hot dog with chili, or a hot dog with sauerkraut. You still have to sell yourself on which one you would like to eat at that time. No matter what the product is or how large or small the product, you still have to sell yourself.

Let's say Mr. Jones is a service manager representative for XYZ company. He took this position because he hates to sell; he hates sales! His boss comes into the service department and states that the company wants him to sell this new product instead of the old product. Mr. Jones looks at the features and realizes that this product is a better product, however it costs two more dollars than the old product. Mr. Jones knows he has to cost justify these features to his customers.

Here's a look at the overall sales process. The product manufacturer had to sell the new product to the CEO of XYZ Company. In turn, the CEO had to sell the features of the product to the district manager, who then sells the product to Mr. Jones' boss, and Mr. Jones' boss has to sell the product to Mr. Jones and his co-workers, and they have to sell the new product to their customers. Welcome to the world of sales!

The price presentation is extremely important and totally determined by you. Keep in mind your competition is out there. You don't want to be too high or too low. Once again look closely at your business plan. Review it carefully. Here is one idea on how to show your price presentation. Make sure the price presentation is clear and easy to understand. I so often see price presentation sheets that are so confusing it would take an electrical engineer or lawyer to figure them out! I also see so many salespeople that can't even figure out their own price presentation sheet. Make sure the price presentation sheet is laminated and included in your presentation book. I have three simple programs. My gold program consists of 50 personal training sessions, my silver program consists of 30 personal training sessions, and my bronze program consists of 20 personal training sessions. The more sessions the lower the price per session. Now that you have given a great orientation, you have come to the final step, the price presentation. Your prospective client explains that he or she will get back to you and thanks you for all of the great information that you have provided. Your mouth drops open, and you freeze! As your jaw thaws you mutter "have a great day," in hope that they will turn around and buy from you. Then you start praying and hope one day they will return. Guess what, they rarely return.

Sales is not simple. It is one of the hardest jobs out there. However, it can be one of the most rewarding jobs today. You will hit this wall, every sales person does. What do you do? The answer is not a simple one. It is called the art of Selling. Being a personal trainer does not make you an order taker. Members are not going to come in bus loads to join. You must understand that people will object, even if they would like to have your service. Prospective clients all want to think about it and talk it over with family and friends.

So what do we do? First, understand the prospective client is going to say something like "thank you, but I want to think about it." Don't be surprised.

Fitness testing is a great tool to use for a potential client. You go through a series of physical tests to establish their baseline fitness level. Then show it to them. If it is poor the client will see where they are compared to the norm. This is something you have not made up, the client did the test and now you can use it in your presentation, explaining that personal training will help them improve their baseline fitness level.

What I like to talk about before we go over objections, is a key ingredient to talk about, "Driving Wants". What is a Driving Want? A Driving Want is the real reason why a person is coming to see you. This is their prime interest. For example, they may say they want to lose weight or for medical reasons. But the real reason why they are here, what motivated them to come, is their hidden agenda or their "Driving Wants". In this example, the person has to lose weight and has medical concerns, but the reason she is there is that she is getting married in six months and wants to look good for her wedding and honeymoon. This is her real reason why she is seeing you. The others are very important but not the real motivation for her to see a personal trainer. You have to be a detective and listen to the client, analyze what they say and sift through all the rubbish to get to the real reason, "The Driving Want". If you don't discover their true Driving Want, you will not get the sale.

Let's get started.

● Objection I: I Want To Think It Over

Steve: Mr. Smith, I can understand that you want to think it over; this is a big decision in your life isn't it? We have talked about your lack of physical activity in the last year and you have shared with me your personal feelings about getting started on an exercise program. You have waited long enough. Let's get started today. Which program would you prefer gold, silver or bronze?

Note: What we have done here is agreed with Mr. Smith's decision. Never disagree. You will lose the battle. Remember to discuss his physical fitness in the last year. Go back and review. And finally, ask for the order again. If you don't get it, go back to your close. Let's get started today. Which program would your prefer gold, silver, or bronze?

- Objection II: I Want To Think It Over – Client is indecisive

Steve: (personal trainer) What exactly do you have to think about?

Mr. Jones: Steve, when making any decision in my life I always go home and think about it.

Steve: I can appreciate this Mr. Jones, when I make a big decision in my life I also have to think it through.

Steve: Mr. Jones, is it the price?

Mr. Jones: No, not the price.

Steve: Mr. Jones is it your wife?

Mr. Jones: No she wants me to get started on an exercise program. She told me about your services.

Steve: Mr. Jones, is it the time?

Mr. Jones: No Steve, I have my own business, I can make my own time.

Steve: Is it me or my services?

Mr. Jones: Steve, I was very impressed with all of your services.

Steve: Then what do you have to think about ?

Mr. Jones: I do have a question on what type of program I will be doing.

Steve: That's great Mr. Jones let me review with you our plans to make you look and feel better (review his program).
Mr. Jones, do you feel comfortable with our services.

Mr. Jones: Oh yes.

Steve: Which program would you prefer? Gold, silver or bronze?

Mr. Jones: I would like the gold program.

Note: In this case I asked what he had to think about. I listen to his reasoning: he doesn't make any decisions until he goes home and thinks about it. I then agreed with Mr. Jones and told him that I do the same thing. I did not disagree with him. Mr. Jones thought he was winning this battle, and
that I was on his side.

This is when I asked him a series of questions to pinpoint what he had to think about. I gave him many outs: Mr.
Jones, is it the price? Is it your wife? Is it time? Is it my services? All of the answers were no. I once again asked a direct question. "Mr. Jones, what do you have to think about?" And finally, Mr. Jones gave me his true objection. He wanted to review his own physical fitness program and compare it to what I can do for him. I then reviewed his program and he had no other objections. We now have Mr. Jones as happy member. You keep closing all of the door of doubt until there are no more open doors.

● Objection 111: I Want To Think It Over – Client is a procrastinator

Steve: Bill, I can appreciate that you want to think it over. We have spent the last hour talking about your physical fitness needs and wants. As you told me, Bill, you have been thinking about getting into shape for one year. Do you have any concerns that I didn't address?

Bill: No Steve, I understand everything, you gave a very good presentation. I just want to think it over a few days.

Steve: I can understand this, Bill. Are you really going to take the time and think about what we discuss?

Bill: Oh yes, I would not be here if I were not serious.

Steve: Bill I have been in this business for more than 35 years. I have talked to many clients like you. Everybody wants to be in the best physical condition. Let me share with you what may happen if you do not get yourself started on an exercise program today. It is now the end of summer. You are thinking that fall and winter is on its way, and you don't have to wear summer clothes. The weather will be bad so why start a personal training program today? Then, Easter rolls around and you can't fit into your suit. You have gained about 20 more pounds from not working out. Then you realize that you should work out and it is summer again and you gained another 20 pounds, and this time your health is failing! You come back and see me 40 pounds heavier, and your doctor is telling you to work out. Bill, you are the closest to ever making a decision on your physical health today. Lets get started. What program would you prefer, gold, silver or bronze?

Bill: I guess you are right Steve. I have been thinking about coming to see you for about a year. I will take the gold program.

Note: In Bill's case, Bill wanted a few days to think it over. I asked him if he was really going to think it over. He said yes, and that he was very serious about getting started on an exercise program. What I did next was to tell a short story about what may happen to him if he does not work out. I knew through the orientation, that he has been thinking about getting started for over one year. Then I explain that he is the closest to ever making a decision on his own personal health. I then went into my closing question, which program would you prefer gold, silver or bronze?

- Objection IV: I Have To Talk To My Wife/ Husband or Significant Other – Client worried about family obligations.

Rose: I really like everything about your personal training program but first I have to go home and discuss this with my husband.

Steve: I can understand that Rose, what do you have to discuss with your husband ?

Rose: Well, Steve, I always talked to him before making any decisions...

Steve: Are you happy and satisfied with our services? .

Rose: Very much so.

Steve: You told me earlier that you want to lose weight by the summer. And that nothing you have done has worked.
Is this correct, Rose?
Rose: Yes, you are right Steve.

Steve: Did your spouse know that you were coming here today?

Rose: Oh yes, he is watching our kids.

Steve: Rose, it seems to me that your spouse is very supportive of what you are doing.

Rose: Oh yes.

Steve: Funny thing about fitness. It is not a concrete object. Fitness is very abstract. Your health is very important to you, however it is more important to your spouse. You are the backbone of your family. You are the family nurse, cook, and family support system. Above all, you are his lover, you are everything. If you get sick due to physical problems such as high blood pressure, or you become overweight, your family is now in jeopardy. You deserve this quality time for yourself and your family. Your spouse would agree to seeing you get started on a personal training program. His encouraging you to come here today shows his support for you. I know he will be very happy with your decision to get started today, so lets get you started. Which program would you prefer? Gold, silver or bronze?

Rose: I will take the bronze program.

Note: In Rose's case she wanted to get started on an exercise program, but wanted to talk to her husband first. Rose, had no objections other than confirmation about getting started. The question that I asked about her husband's support was very important. The turning point was her response, "Yes, my husband is watching our kids." I then explained the value of her being the backbone of the family and that her husband's action of watching the kids showed support of what she was doing. Having all these "doors" closed, I proceeded with my closing sequence. Which program would you prefer gold, silver or bronze?

● Objection V: I Have To Talk To My Spouse – Client worried about spending the money

Sam: Steve I like everything about your program, however, I always talk to my wife before making any major decisions.

Steve: I can understand that Sam, I have to discuss major items with my wife also. What exactly do you have to discuss with your spouse.

Sam: I just want her OK.

Steve: I can understand that, Sam. Is it the money?

Sam: Oh no, I have my own money and she has her own money.

Steve: Do you have to ask your spouse to go out to get your hair cut?

Sam: Oh no, Steve.

Steve: Do you have to ask your spouse to go out to eat?

Sam: No, I go out for lunch everyday.

Steve: That's great. Sam, does your spouse ask you when she could go out to lunch?

Sam: No, Steve.

Steve: Does your spouse ask you when she gets her nails and hair done?

Sam: No.

Steve: Sam in today's society, with two people working you have a little freedom to use some of your money for personal use. Do you agree, Sam?

Sam: Yes

Steve: I realize that as a family you must make major decisions together. For example when buying a television you will both be watching it. So, purchasing the television becomes a joint decision. Buying carpets requires you both agree on the color. However, fitness is a little different.
Looking good and feeling good can be obtained through fitness. Fitness is an individual decision. Going to get your hair cut is for you. When you go out to eat, this is for you.
Fitness is only for you. The result is that it can make you feel better and look better, which in turn will make your spouse and your family feel better about you. This affects everybody. Take some of your lunch money and put it towards your new body. Because the lunches are killing you!

Sam: Steve, you are right, I do spend x amount of money each day on my lunches and coffee breaks. I can use some of this money for me. My spouse gets her hair done, and nails done. I guess she would not mind me using my own money for getting in shape.

Steve: Just re-organize your money for lunch and prioritize your needs. Your lunches are destroying you. Use the additional savings and let's get you back in shape. Which program would you prefer? Gold, silver or bronze?

Sam: Let me start off with your silver program.

Steve: That's great, let's get started!

Note: In Sam's case, I first agreed with Sam about talking major decisions with his spouse. Then I asked Sam if it was the money. Sam said he has his own money, and his wife has hers. I then asked Sam if he had to ask his spouse to get a haircut or go to lunches. Sam said no. I asked if his spouse needed to ask Sam to go to lunch or get her nails or hair done, and the answer was also no. What I did was establish the point that he and his spouse each determine how to spend their own money. Then I explained that there are joint decisions and individual decisions. Health is an individual decision that will positively affect everyone. Then I showed Sam that he can use some of his lunch money for our personal training program, ending with the closing question, "which program do you prefer, gold, silver or bronze?" The two turning points of this case were that Sam has his own money, and that Sam spent money everyday to buy his lunch. I knew he could afford this program because he was spending additional money every day, this can also include smoking cigarettes and drinking alcohol. All things you don't need to survive

● Objection VI: I Can't Afford It/price Objection

Judy: Steve, I really want to get started on your program but I can't afford an added expense at this time.

Steve: Judy, I can understand this. Is it only the money?

Judy: Oh yes, I like your program, Steve.
Steve: Judy, let's take a look at why you came here today. You want to lose about 30 pounds and bring down your stress level, is that correct?
Judy: Yes

Steve: Money is required in almost everything we do in today's society, do you agree Judy?

Judy: Yes

Steve: Let's take a look at how I can help you get involved in our program. You would like to lose 30 pounds and bring down your stress level. The nice part of our program is that the money you spend is totally for you, and no one else. This may sound selfish, but when is the last time you spent money on you?
Judy: I went to the movies, with my girlfriends, and then out to dinner.

Steve: That's great. How did you feel?

Judy: I had a great time, but we did talk about our friend John who just had a heart attack.

Steve: Is John OK!

Judy: Oh yes, he is now in rehabilitation.

Steve: Judy, the funny thing about health and fitness, is that one cannot put a price on it. Fitness is not materialistic. It is a state of mind. It will help you release stress at work, and it is an avenue toward feeling good and looking good which will help you loose your 30 pounds. Most of all it is preventive medicine so you don't end up in rehab or in a hospital with problems like heart attack, high blood pressure, weight and stress problems. Wouldn't you agree?

Judy: Yes, I would get started today, but I can't afford the gold program at this time.

Steve: Do you like the gold program?

Judy: It is the most affordable but I just do not have the full amount.

Steve: Judy, this is what I can do for you. I will give you the gold program because it is our best program. If I break down the gold program into monthly dues without interest will this help?

Judy: Oh yes.

Steve: That's great. Lets get started on your gold program today.

Note: In Judy's case, she liked our program and could afford it with a little budgeting and financing assistance. She used the objection that she could not afford our program. I had to find out why, and how I could get her started. First, I reviewed her original goal to lose 30 pounds and reduce stress. Then I asked her when she spent money on herself.
She related going to the movies and dinner with her friends.
This is when I found out about her friend John who just had a heart attack. I then explained the benefits of fitness and the added benefit of preventive medicine. The true objection came out when she said she liked the gold program but could not afford to pay for the program in full. This is when I said that I could help her with monthly dues, without interest.

Notice I did not go to a lesser program such as silver or bronze, because I knew in the long run it would cost Judy more money per session and this was not the best value for her! I then showed her how she could afford our most cost- effective program by simply making small monthly payments without interest.

● Objection VII: I Can't Afford It/price Objection – Client using cost as an excuse

Frank: I like everything you said. I just cannot afford this program at this time. Thank you very much for your time. I will let all my friends know about your services. Thank you and have a great day.

Steve: Frank, I am glad that you like my services. What exactly are you going to tell your friends about my services?

Frank: You are very knowledgeable and your program is very sound. And the price is reasonable.

Steve: I can understand that. Is there anything you don't like about my service.

Frank: Oh no, I would take your program in a minute if I could afford it.

Steve: Do you go out with your friends to a pub, or a bar?
Frank: Once a week, just for a few drinks.

Steve: That's great. Being single, do you do any other activities during the week?

Frank: Once a week I play on a volleyball coed team, and on Sundays I play softball with my company team.

Steve: Frank, that's great. What position do you play in your company softball team?

Frank: Right field.

Steve: Frank, how important is it that you do well during your volleyball coed team, and your softball team?

Frank: It's not that important, I just do it to meet other women, and have fun.

Steve: I can understand that Frank. Would it make a difference if you were able to perform better in your sports?

Frank: Oh, it doesn't hurt.

Steve: It sounds as if you have a very active social life.

Frank: And that's only part of it. I love to go bowling with my dad on Wednesday nights.

Steve: Who wins most of the bowling games?

Frank: We generally split most of the games.

Steve: Frank, I realize that you came here to see what our services offer and how it can benefit you.

Frank: I really like your services, Steve, I just cannot afford it at this time.

Steve: I understand, Frank. Let me clarify a few things. Do you like our services? Is there any thing you don't like about me?

Frank: Oh, Steve, I really like your services, and I like you.
I just cannot afford it at this time.

Steve: If we were able to make your life better would you consider our program?

Frank: Of course, who wouldn't?

Steve: Frank I realize that you are involved in many activities. I give you credit. The one thing I can offer you is. .
Frank: What's that?

Steve: It seems to me that you really enjoy all your social activities. These activities may or may not cost you any money. Do you agree?

Frank: That's correct, what are you getting at?

Steve: Frank, you seem to be in good shape, and you seem to enjoy playing volleyball and softball and once a week going bowling with your dad. If I can take three hours a week and have you exercise, this will help you become a little stronger, which in turn, will help improve your strength in hitting the volleyball harder, having a better throwing arm, and hitting a softball harder and possibly hitting more home runs. Most of all, you will have the endurance to be able to bowl with more strength and control, possibly winning more games against your dad. Would this be worth it?

Frank: I always wanted to beat my dad in bowling. If I could hit a couple more home runs this year it may open up more corporate doors. Looking better and hitting the volleyball better may even improve my social life.

Steve: So let's get started.

Frank: Steve, I would love to but I just can't afford it. Thanks anyway.

Steve: Frank, you just agreed that this program can help you in your sports and your social life. Do you agree?

Frank: Yes.
Steve: If you look at all the different activities that you are doing and break it down, personal training will help not one but all of your social activities. What program can offer you all of this?

Frank: I do agree. I just can't afford it at this time.

Steve: Franks is it really the money ?

Frank: Steve I am involved in so many things right now, I really don't know if I can afford another expense.

Steve: We have agreed that this expense will help all of your other activities?

Frank: Oh, yes.

Steve: If you break down our cost of x amount into improving your social life, improving your volleyball, softball, bowling, and most of all looking better and feeling better, you can see personal training can better your entire life, not just one part of it. Which program would you prefer, Frank, gold, silver or bronze?

Frank: I am not totally sold on this idea.

Steve: How can I help you?

Frank: Can I work out in the evening?

Steve: What time would you like to work out?

Frank: 8:00 PM on Sunday night?

Steve: I do have an opening at 8:00 PM on Sunday.

Frank: What do I have to bring ?

Steve: Just yourself, I will do the rest.

Frank: OK, Steve, I would like to try this. It may sound crazy but I will pay by the session. And I know it is the most expensive way to go, but if I like it I will then decide what program I would like to do. Is that okay?

Steve: That's great. Frank. I will see you this Sunday at 8:00 PM.

Note: In Frank's case he liked our program, and wanted to tell all of his friends. He thought this would get him off the hook. I then asked what he would tell his friends about our program. I knew he couldn't say anything negative, because he just told me how much he liked the program. I then asked Frank about his social life. Frank seemed to have a very heavy schedule: drinking once a week with his friends, coed volleyball, his company softball team, etc. I asked Frank twice about working out, if it would help his game. First, "how important is it that you do well during your volleyball coed team, and your softball team?" His answer, "not that important." Second, "would it make a different if you were able to perform better in your sports?" His answer, "it doesn't hurt," which is a somewhat positive statement. I then asked Frank again if he really liked our services, and if he really liked me. Once again Frank was very positive. He explained to me for the fourth time that he could not afford it. I then explained to him that all of his activities seemed to be very important to him. I showed how fitness would improve all of his sports, not just one. I then asked Frank if it really was the money. And after stating for the sixth time that he could not afford it, the real objection came out. He was involved in so many activities that he really didn't know two things: how to fit it into his schedule, and if it would be cost effective.

I once again reinforced the benefits of fitness and went into a closing sequence. He then explained that he still wasn't sold. He wanted a certain time. I gave him the time he wanted.

If I did not have this time available, I would give him the closest time to what he requested. Frank wanted to pay by the session. This is funny! To pay by the session is the most expense way. Obviously, money wasn't the issue at all. It was never an issue. The real concern was time.

• Objection VIII: I Can't Afford It/Price Objection – Client has doctors order, needs counseling to find funds in budget

Joe: Steve, I like your program. I just cannot afford it. It costs too much.

Steve: Joe, how much is too much?

Joe: The total cost is just to high.

Steve: Joe, your doctor sent you here because of your high blood pressure and sedentary life style. Am I correct?

Joe: Yes, but it is too expensive.

Steve: Let me break this down for you. You pay seven dollars a pack for cigarettes, and you smoke two packs per day. This equals ninety-eight dollars per week, four hundred twenty five dollars per month, and five thousand and one hundred dollars per year, all to destroy your body. Now let's add your drinking once a week with your poker club, a low estimate of fifteen dollars per week. This equals seven hundred and eighty dollars per year. The total for just smoking and drinking alone is $5,880 per year. Joe, you spend well over $5,000 destroying your body. Now, I know our services will help you. And Joe, our program is half the cost. So lets get started. The doctor did order this.

Joe: I guess you are right. What are your programs again?
Steve: There's the gold, silver or bronze. Which would you prefer?

Joe: I will take the gold program.

Steve: That's great. I will call your doctor today and ask him for additional health information. I will see you on Friday at 12:00 noon.

Note: In Joe's case, the doctor already sent him to see me. I told Joe how much money he was spending on items that were destroying his life. You can also include junk food and fast food as additional costs. It is amazing how much people spend on items to destroy their bodies. The total is so much more than the cost of personal training.

● Objection IX: Time Objection

Sue: I like your program very much Steve. My biggest problem is time.

Steve: Sue, time is precious, and I agree with you. I wish there were 30 hours in the day instead of 24 but I would probably fill 30 hours up if I had them. Sue, if your doctor told you that you must come for treatments to help your heart condition or you will die, would you make the time?

Sue: Of course. But fitness and health is not life or death.

Steve: Sue, I do agree. However, if you don't start exercising now you may end up with health problems in the future which can be life threatening. Let's prevent you from becoming ill, now.

Sue: I have such a tight schedule I don't know when I can fit this in.

Steve: Let me help you find a way. Out of a 5 day work weeks what day is good for you?

Sue: Friday night.

Steve: That's great, how about six at night?

Sue: Six would be fine. How long are these work-outs?

Steve: I would put aside an hour to an hour and a half, at the most.

Sue: So, Steve what you are saying is that I only need to come here about 3 days a week for a total of only 3 hours.

Steve: That's correct.

Sue: I thought I had to work out for hours on end.
Steve: No Sue, that's the beauty of fitness. For only 3 hours a week 3 times a week this program will help you prevent any type of health problems: heart problems, high blood pressure, etc. And Sue, this program will help you look better and also feel better-two more added assists and features. Do you have a day free during the weekend?

Sue: I have Sunday nights free.

Steve: I have an opening at 7:00 PM.

Sue: That will be great!

Steve: Let me just clarify for myself. I have you down for a work-out on Friday night at 6:00 PM And Sunday night at 7:00 PM Is there any other time during the week or week- end that is good for you?

Sue: Thinking about it, I don't have to be in work on Tuesday until 2:00 PM Do you have any time before 2:00
PM on Tuesday ?

Steve: I do have an opening at 11:00   AM on Tuesday.

Sue: That will work into my schedule perfectly.

Steve: Let me just review, I have you scheduled for Friday 6:00 PM, Sunday 7:00 PM and Tuesday 1 1:00 AM. Is this correct?

Sue: Yes Steve.

Steve: If you have to make any changes in your schedule don't hesitate to call. I can always work around your schedule. Sue, which program would you prefer? Gold, silver, or bronze?

Sue: I will take the gold program and bring you the check on Friday at 6:00 PM

Steve: Great! I am looking forward to seeing you on Friday.

Note: In Sue's case she was very up front with her problem.
It was not the money, it was simply the time. I showed her how she could work out 3 days a week for only 3 hours. Sue did not realize how easy fitness and working out can be. I also explained about the added benefits of looking good and feeling good. Then I helped her with her workout time.
First, I broke it down to a 5 day week, added the weekend, and asked her to look at her 7 day schedule. All along I was reinforcing and confirming her appointments with me. Being a personal trainer you are there for your clients. You may have to work nights, holidays or weekends. At the end, I went into my closing sequence: which program do you prefer?

● Objection X: Will I Stick With It?

Ralph: Steve, I like your program, however I know myself.
Every time I start something, I simply quit. I like it for the first
month or so, then I just give up.

Steve: This is not uncommon, Ralph. What type of activities or
sports do you always quit?

Ralph; I play football in the winter and in the summer I play
baseball.

Steve; Do you enjoy playing these sports?

Ralph: Sometimes. I lose interest and I guess you can't call it
quitting, because I do finish the seasons. I just simply lose interest.

Steve: Ralph, what you are playing are team sports. Winning or
losing is not solely predicated on you. Am I correct?

Ralph: I never thought about it; I guess you are right.

Steve: The best part about fitness is that the only one who wins is
you! The great part about fitness is that you can see changes in a
short period of time.

Ralph: What do you mean, Steve?

Steve: You will feel positive changes in your mental attitude right
away. You will have more vim and vigor. It will take
approximately 4 to 6 months to see physical changes. The best
thing about this, Ralph, is that we can chart your progress. Let's
say when we start you can only ride a bike for three minutes. I will
help you to do better. And you will see your own progress. This is

why so many people love to exercise. Ralph, again, this is for you. This is not a team effort.

Ralph: Steve, I never realized this.

Steve: What program will you prefer? Gold, silver or bronze?

Ralph: Not so fast! I know you can chart my progress. I still feel that when I start I will not finish, or I will lose interest.

Steve: Ralph, I can understand this; we are not all machines or computers. We are human beings with moods, feelings, and different activities that change every day in our lives.
You will have days that you will not be able to make it. I do realize this. You may have holidays, sickness, personal problems etc. But why did you come here?

Ralph: To get back to a size 32 waistline.

Steven: You thought about coming here, did you not?

Ralph: Yes I see your sign every day as I go to work.

Steve: I can't and won't promise you the world, I can't make any guarantees. The only thing I can say, Ralph, is that fitness   does work. And if you put in a little time and effort, the payoff is remarkable. You will look better, feel better and best of all, I will try to get you back into your size 32 pants. You have to do your part. Simply come to me 3 days a week for only 1 hour and watch your diet. I will do the rest.

Ralph: How about if I miss?

Steve: I am sure that you will miss occasionally, and that is okay. We have seven days in a week we can always reschedule.

Ralph: It seems too simple.

Steve: Ralph, the hardest part was to walk into my office. To make the commitment to do an activity for you and not your team. With a smaller waistline and additional strength, you may even improve in your sports.

Ralph: I guess you are right Steve. What were the programs again?

Steve: We have a gold, silver and bronze program.

Ralph: Is there a time limit that I have to use up in these sessions?

Steve: That's a great question. The answer is no.

Ralph: I get penalized if I have to reschedule?

Steve: No, not with a 24 hour notice. If less than 24 hours notice there is a fee.

Ralph: What happens if I get very sick or injured?

Steve: Ralph, this is not school, you don't have to bring me in a doctor's note. What I will do for you is freeze your pro- gram until you are ready to come back.

Ralph: Steve, I guess you answered all of my questions and concerns. Let's get started on that gold program.

Steve: That's great. I will see you Sunday at 12:00.

Note: In Ralph's case I explained that weight lifting is not a team sport. Fitness is an individual sport. And fitness will only help him.

I showed Ralph how fitness can improve his mental state and how long it will take to improve his physical state. I then went for a trial close. What program would you prefer? Gold, silver or bronze? But Ralph's reply was not so fast.

I explained that we are not all computers. And that it is okay if we do miss some work-outs. I then reaffirmed that his original goal was to have a 32 inch waistline. I showed him if he can come into my studio 3 times a week for just one hour, I will do the rest. I explained that the hardest thing Ralph did was to walk into my office, and make a commitment towards fitness.

I again asked for the order or the close. Ralph then asked a number of questions in regard to time. I answered all of his questions and concerns. I then set up an appointment to work out.

Make sure you know your policies and procedures inside and out. If you stumble and seem not to know, you will lose that client. He or she will be thinking you made it up as you went along.

● Objection XI: Don't Pressure Me!

Steve: Jim, we have talk about your lack of physical activity Your doctor told you to come here or you will have continued health problems. You have used every excuse in the book not to get started. What is the real reason why you don't want to get started today?

Jim: I don't like to be pressured into making any decisions. This is my body and I will take as long as necessary to make a decision.

Steve: I can understand that Jim, however let me tell you what pressure is. Pressure is seeing your wife and children looking at you in your coffin. That's pressure! Because your doctor is telling you to get into shape and if you don't, this is where you will end up. So let's stop making excuses and let's get started.

Jim: Steve, you are truly tough and I like that. I suppose I needed a kick in the butt. I will see you Monday, and here is my check for the gold program.

Note: In Jim's case this is done at the very end of a very long presentation. This is a very bold close. It will go only two ways, Jim will join or Jim will walk out your office. No other way. Sometimes you have to be very bold. Brutally honest!

- Objection XII: I Can Get a Gym Membership for $10 to $20 a month

Wendy: Steve, I can buy a gym membership for $10 a month, it has all the equipment I need to work out with.

Steve: Wendy, this may be true that you get a membership for $10 a month, however as the old saying goes, "you get what you pay for". Yes you get the equipment, but that is all you get. This does not come with supervision or very limited supervision. It doesn't come with a program, or a very generic one. With me, you get total one on one personal training for an hour, with my undivided attention. We will go over your diet and exercise program. All these gyms are popping up everywhere, they work on the premise that you don't come to the gym and they get your money. I work on the premise that you have to come to the gym to get results. So let's get started today.

Wendy: I can get started at the end of the week with the Gold Program. Do you take PayPal?

Steve: Yes.

A final note: as you can see, the world of closing a sale is very complex. My friend Dave Popivchak once told me that closing is when you are in a room with several open doors, and your job is to close every one of these doors. If you leave one door open you will loose the sale. If you close all the doors you have done your job and now you have a new client, and a very happy client because you addressed all of his or her concerns and questions. This will lessen buyer's remorse.

I feel very strongly that to be a great Personal Trainer, you must learn the art of closing a sale. We have a great number of personal trainers who are very knowledgeable, and highly educated. But we are losing the battle and leaving the field because personal trainers can't or don't know how to close a sale. You must be skilled in answering objections such as "I want to think it over, I have to talk to my husband, I have to talk to my wife, the program costs to much." Closing a sale is an art and the only way you learn this art is by educating yourself and by true experiences.

Closing a sale can be a lot of fun and the rewards are plentiful, the client wins and you win. Start practicing with friends and family. Then go out and close a sale. You will see your income increase.

Service & Rules for Success

You are #1

Rule #67: Have Fun!

On The Road To Success:

54 Rules To Help You Succeed

Rule 1: Safety Should Be Number #1

You should always protect your clients' and your own safety. Accidents do happen. To prevent accidents you must keep all of your equipment well maintained. Inspect your equipment once a week and log it. If you're in a gym situation let the management know if there are any maintenance problems. Just by taking 30 minutes out of your day to inspect equipment you can prevent a serious injury and a possible lawsuit.

Also, keep in mind your members and your own safety when it comes to traveling to or from a training session. In cases of severe weather conditions or other natural disasters, you should cancel all sessions so not to put anyone in harms way.

Rule 2: Service, Service, Service

Service is the key. This is what separates you from every- body else. Your service will make you or break you even if you have done everything else; your homework, your advertising, client orientation. **Service alone creates obligation**. Don't ever forget this. Great service does not cost you. It pays you generously! Poor service can cost you clientele and your reputation.

Rule 3: Treat Each Client Differently

Remember, every case is different. I feel that every client I train has a different goal and a different journey. Every client has a different disposition. I see many personal trainers treat every client exactly the same. I thought I was watching a production line when watching some trainers doing the same thing over and over again. Service your members with totally independent goals. Each and every one of your clients has a different story and a different journey to travel. You cannot treat everyone as the same. You are not running an assembly line work out. A lot of gyms have circuit weight training stations that anyone can do. But are they getting results? Are they getting attention? Are they getting supervision? Are they getting new information? Are they getting one on one interaction? The answer to all of these is NO! You are the one that makes the difference; you are the key to your client's success. Each client does have his/her journey to undertake, however the key is this is your journey too. This adventure is an awesome one for you and your clients. Have fun and enjoy the ride.

Rule 4: Knowing the Fine Line Between a Great workout and an Extremely Hard, Exhausting No Fun workout.

In the opening of this book I talk about who needs personal trainers. Members get a better workout from a personal trainer than they can get at home or at a gym. You have to make every one of your clients realize this. For example, John was doing 4 sets of 10 repetitions with 225 lb. on the bench press. You may have him do 5 sets of 10 reps with 225 lbs. on the bench press, changing one variable (the sets) and John could feel great. However, if you change more than one variable, and have John doing 5 sets of 15 reps with 230 1bs, he could feel that you have worked him too hard and may not want to use your service.

You will lose your clients this way. However, you will never hear about it. Your clients may use other excuses for not training with you. They'll tell you their work schedule changed. They're training with their training partner again.
Their spouse needs them at home. That they feel you worked them too hard will never be mentioned. To prevent this from happening

you must constantly ask your clients questions throughout your session to see how he or she is feeling. Feedback will always keep you in sink with the training.

Rule 5: Ask Questions About Their Workouts

There is no limit on how many questions you can ask throughout a workout. This indicates that you are listening to the client and assures that you and your client are on the same page. Keep in mind during the whole questioning process their Driving Wants. Here are just a few questions you should ask during their workout:

- Are the weights too heavy?
- Do you feel that you can do another set?
- Do you feel dizzy? Does your stomach feel upset?
- Would you like something to drink?
- Is the heat (or air conditioning) to cold or too hot?
- Do you feel any sharp pains?

Rule 6: Ask Questions About Their Social Lives

Show that you are interested in them by asking about their social lives, ie: How was the concert, or how was your vacation? How are their children? People love to talk about themselves and their lives.

Rule 7: Never Make Guarantees

I have come across so many personal trainers who guarantee that their members will get results. You cannot predict what a person will or will not do after leaving your training session. They can go home and eat an entire pizza and tell you the next day that they had a salad for dinner. Never guarantee your work. What you can guarantee is that fitness and diet do work, and that it will take a long period of time. It took a long time to get out of shape and it will take a long time to get into shape.

Tell your clients that if they do their part with their diet, you will do your part in the exercise portion and they will see results. You cannot guarantee what they will be. But they will be better than what they started with. They will feel better, loose inches and pounds. For example, I had a gentleman come into my office and ask me if he would increase his bench press by thirty pounds working out with me. I told him there are no guarantees at all but with hard work we can see what we can do. Always be honest with your client from the start and not make any guarantees. They can come back and bite you. A client who only lose 20 pounds will be upset if you had told her she would lose 30 pounds, so do not guarantee results.

Rule 8: When Working with Your Clients Stay With Them and Don't Leave Their Sight

I remember seeing a personal trainer spend one hour with a client, by putting him on a bike and then returning one hour later after the client had paid for the entire session. You may laugh and think this doesn't happen. If I did not witness this myself I would not believe it. This person was paying a personal trainer for not being there. This was not an isolated incident; I have seen many other cases. I remember seeing a personal trainer talking to her boyfriend for half an hour while training a client, not paying any attention to her client at all.

Rule 9: Don't be a beached whale

I have seen trainers sitting or even laying on a resist-a-ball training clients. You should always be standing and interacting with your members. Posture and body language tells a lot about a trainer.

Rule 10: Don't allow your friends to join in your clients session.

I saw a personal trainer having his friends work out with the client he was training Remember, it should be you and your client and no one else. This is what they are paying you for.

Rule 11: Talk to Your Clients In Simple Terms

I have seen many personal trainers who think they are doctors. They talk as if their clients know all the medical terms of the body and muscle groups.

You may use medical terminology. "Bob, you are working the gastronemius muscle." In layman's terms that refers to the calf muscle. I have worked with doctors who did not know the anatomical terminology for certain muscles. Keep everything in layman's terms. If a client asks you about a certain exercise and what specific muscle it works, then you may want to explain the medical and technical terms.
Remember: People want to know how much you care before they care how much you know. Impress them once they realize just how much you care. So keep it simple.

Rule 12: Let Your Clients Talk About Themselves

Keep in mind this is your client's hour and not yours. I have seen personal trainers take up the entire hour talking about themselves, their personal problems or their social life. Don't forget-you are working for your client. They are not working for you. This time is for your client. They may use this time to relax or to talk about their day or night and some- times vent their anger or stress level. The more it is about them and not you the more clients you will have.

Rule 13: Know Your Members Preference, Music or No Music during workouts

This is not your hour, it is their hour. To make it more enjoyable for my clients, I have over 1,000 cd's they can choose from. If not, they can bring in their own Ipod and play whatever music they like. This will also enhance their workouts and make them very enjoyable. I work long days but it is all about them. Even if you are at the end of a 13 hour day, and the client has music you don't like, you put it on for them, not for you. They will tell their friends what they are experiencing in a very positive manor.

Rule 14: Always Take a Shower Or Smell Good Before A Training Session

I recall seeing a personal trainer come in from his 12 mile run and go right into a personal training session. Let me tell you something. He was sweating from head to toes. He was sweating all over and around his client and boy did he smell. This was very disturbing to me and I know it was very disturbing to his client. This is a great way to lose business!

Rule 15: Always Brush Your Teeth Or Use Mouth Wash Before A Training Session

There was a time when I was working with other personal trainers. One trainer went to see a client immediately after eating a salad with onions. The woman almost fell to the ground every time he spoke to her. It was terrible to witness and worse, I'm sure, for his client to smell. I felt so sorry for her. She never did come back. And the personal trainer had no idea why. Again, a great way to decrease your income and clientele.

Rule 16: Don't overuse cologne or perfume

Too much cologne or perfume can be disruptive to your member's workout. It can also steer people away from you. Additionally, some people may have allergies to various scents.

Rule 17: Always Dress Very Professionally

I knew of a personal trainer who was very knowledgeable and highly educated. He didn't have many clients because he always dressed in very old soiled sweat suits and he had a very bad body odor. I told him in a very nice way to "clean up his act." He took my advise and he is very successful now. He looks like a million dollars, and smells like a cologne commercial. His income and clientele increased.

Rule 18: Cleanliness

Many clients will never tell you. I have seen trainers lose clients because of this. This can seriously hinder your success. You MUST keep a clean studio. Make sure your health club is clean. Make sure your bathrooms, showers, equipment, mirrors, ceilings, and of course your office, are all clean! If you keep a dirty studio, or work out in a dirty gym, or have a dirty office, it reflects poorly on your ability as a trainer. In plain English, dirt will kill you your business. That means you will lose money! It only takes 30 minutes out of your day to keep your office or studio clean. Just do it!

Rule 19: Always bring in new equipment and update old

You should constantly change your equipment to enhance your gym. This may be as easy as adding a new kettle bell or as complex as getting a new elliptical. Change is good and keeps your clients talking. Always make sure your equipment is well maintained.

Rule 20: Always be Ready to Start

Always be at the front desk or standing waiting by the door for your client, old or new. I see so many clients waiting for their personal trainer at the front desk, wasting their valuable time.

Rule 21: Always Be Prompt

When you travel to your client's location, whether it be their house, gym or company, make sure you allow sufficient travel time. Remember there may be delays you can't prevent such as bad weather, accidents, traffic delays, etc. Give yourself extra time just in case.

Note: You will have to factor this time into your total price. But don't be late. Being late can cause you to lose your credibility and, possibly, your client. Remember that the important thing is your client's schedule and not yours. If you are late this can affect your client's entire schedule which can cause them a lot of trouble. They may decide that it isn't worth having you as a trainer because you are late and if your lateness costs them money you will be out the door in a minute.

Rule 22: Visualize before the workout

Just like when a professional athlete is going to perform an athletic task they visualize what they are going to do prior to the event. You as a trainer should visualize your entire workout prior to the client's arrival. For example, know your warm up program, the actual program and what you are going to do as a cool down.

Rule 23: Be organized

Organization is the key to your success in both paperwork and workout area. Make sure you know where everything is in your gym. It will make you look very unprofessional if you have to look around for something you need for the workout. This will also prevent injuries due to equipment not being where they should be.

Rule 24: Do Not Try to Sell Any Products To Your Clients
I once saw a personal trainer, who while training her client, would talk about her other business selling vacations. She was trying to talk her client into purchasing a vacation from her. The client did not seem interested at all. Remember, you are here to train your clients, not to sell your products.

Rule 25: Don't Show Off

I have seen so many trainers run faster than their clients and lift more weight than their clients. This can lead to the trainer falling, or dropping the weights, and embarrassing them- selves. This is an excellent way to lose clients. Remember, don't show off in front of your clients. Members don't care what you can do, they are only interested in what you can do for them.

Rule 26: Do Not Workout with Clients

I have seen personal trainers do an entire workout with a client and also I have seen personal trainers who spot, observe and correct proper technique in lifting. Working out with the client takes away from the client's time and takes the focus off of them and on to you. (NOTE: if you are training several clients throughout the day it can over tax your body). Remember, they are paying for your time and expertise, not for you to get a workout.

Rule 27: Be Creative

A very big part of personal training is your creativity. Be creative. There are no limits and no rules. I remember watching a TV program where there was a poker game going on. I think it was an old John Wayne western. The next client I had was a very young, strong and beautiful model, She loved to be physically tested to her highest potential. This young woman loved to work her abdominal. So I brought down a deck of cards and explained that each card represents how many sit-ups she would be doing. And the face cards represent 10 leg raises for jacks, 20 leg raises for queens, and 30 leg raises for kings. Aces and jokers are worth 50 crunches each. She had a great work out and loved it!

Rule 28: Use theme workouts

I had a member bring in sand, palm trees and a small pool and we had a "Beach" workout. You can do this for a day, week or month. Members love this.

Rule 29: Current Events

Always be aware of current events. To make workouts interesting you can incorporate what is happening in the world. For example, when the great boxing legend, Joe Frazier passed away I had boxing workouts with each of my clients in his honor.

Rule 30: Don 't Be Afraid to Ask for Help

Being a professional is knowing when to ask for assistance. When you consult with a doctor, physical therapist, chiropractor or another personal trainer, they will appreciate that you are asking questions to help your client. This can also get you more business because it shows that you care about your clients. I have talked to a

lot of personal trainers who feel that they're working for themselves when their first
concern should be their clients.

If you don't know the answer, ask. There are so many personal trainers who think they know it all, they are afraid to ask for any help, or feel that asking for help would be a blow to their pride. They would not want their client to find out, I love to ask questions. This makes me a better trainer. I don't claim to know everything about personal training. I am always open for suggestions and help. Additional education and knowledge only makes you a better trainer.

Rule 31: This is Not a 9 to 5 Job

You can not be "off" weekends and holidays. If you don't agree with this, you are in the wrong business. Being a personal trainer means that you are going to be working on holidays, weekends, during the very early morning-sometimes 5 am to as late as 11 pm. You have to work when it is most convenient for your clients. If you don't like what I am saying, this may not be the business for you. Clients come first, not you.

Rule 32: Don't Be A Watchdog!

I've seen hundreds of personal trainers in my lifetime. I managed several personal trainers in a fortune 500 corporation. What I noticed was that each personal trainer has their own personality. The trainers that were most successful were the ones who would not look at their watches. They would not book too many personal training sessions in a day. They would spend over an hour with their clients and not stop on the hour, giving a little bit more time than the other trainers. You will be surprised on how this can increase your business. Members will talk highly of you. That extra time will get you extra members and extra income.

If you have an hour session scheduled, give your member an hour and a half and watch what happens. You will have a very satisfied member who will tell the world about you. I advertise an hour workout in my ads, but I give as much as a half hour extra to everyone depending on their fitness level.

Rule 33: Always Leave a Workout on a Positive Note

Always accentuate the positive in a workout. Never end on a negative or sour note. Remember, your clients should leave smiling and glad you were there for them. Even if they had a bad workout there is always something positive to say at the end, such as, I am so glad you made it. Yes it was a tough workout but the tougher you are the better you will be. Every step you make, no matter how small, is a step getting you closer to your goal.

Rule 34: Homework

There will be times, if not every session, that I will give homework. Homework can be as simple as having them take pictures of themselves, watching a video on weightlifting. It may also be giving written assignments about a certain subject. Believe it or not, as crazy as it may sound, my clients love homework. NOTE: it keeps them wanting to come back. It is also great for feedback and discussion. For example, I had someone write a paper of the dangers of steroids and the next session we discussed it. One of your many roles as a personal trainer is that of a teacher. The more you teach your clients, the more they will come back.

Rule 35: Have Different Types of People as Clients

There are too many personal trainers who are one dimensional. They will only work with a certain clientele. There are personal trainers who work with only volleyball players. You should be able to work with all different types of people. This will help to make you well rounded.

Working with different clients makes your day more interesting and a lot of fun. I have been an AAU Olympic Weightlifting official, an AAU Powerlifting official and an AAU Bodybuilding official. All of these facets allow me to have a larger client base which includes Olympic lifters, Power lifters and Bodybuilders.

Don't be afraid to work with clients who are very over- weight, handicapped, sick, elderly or children over the age of 12. (With these clients, make sure you get a medical clearance) Each and every one of us needs some assistance at some time in our lives. We are here to serve anyone who needs us, not only the Healthy and Wealthy!

Rule 36: Be a chameleon

There may be times where you have a routine set up for your client and for some reason the client comes in with a different frame of mind or attitude. You may have to totally change your program around to fit this person's needs. For example I had a weightlifting plan for a member and he came in very agitated and angry. I totally changed his program to boxing so he could let out his anger and aggression on the fly. He loved it and it was one of his best workouts. He thanked me for changing his routine.

Another example, your member has had a very bad day at the office and you had planned on doing x amount of weight on the bench press. Explain to your client that because they are not mentally ready to do a 1 rep movement (rm), or 100 percent maximum weight, you'd like to try working their cardio and do a circuit weight training program today instead. Always have two or three additional workouts in your head. Just incase you have to change the workout.

Rule 37: Don't Be a Jack of All Trades, Master of None

I know so many trainers who do more than one job. For example, a personal trainer during the day and a waiter at night. They focus on everything except being the best personal trainer they can be. How could they expect to be successful? If you want to be a successful personal trainer you have to walk the walk, not just talk the talk. Your clients expect nothing less and deserve nothing less!

Rule 38: Always Be Confidential

This is very, very important! You must keep all of your clients' personal information totally confidential. I have files on each and every client. No one is allowed to look at these files without the client's permission. Keep in mind that is why we call this field Personal Training. Make sure you have before-and- after photos of your clients. Get their permission in writing to show their picture. Betrayal of your clients' trust can ruin your business. Have your files locked up.

Rule 39: Waivers and Release forms

You can either go to an attorney or you can go online and find basic waivers to protect yourself. You should have every member sign one for working out. Also, a waiver for the use of their picture for your website, advertising, etc.

Rule 40: Education is the Key to Your Success

Never stop learning. Education is fun. Book knowledge is very good but application and lifetime experiences are far more important. It is imperative that you continue your education in one form or another. Education will make you sharp and stronger mentally. Take classes in fitness, read a book on fitness once a month, review and watch videos, read fitness magazines and articles. Search the Internet for information on subjects dealing with fitness. Would you like to know more about plyometrics? Do a research paper on plyometrics. Give demonstrations. Pick a subject once a month and you will find that you will have a great time exploring and learning about new or old fitness subjects.

Rule 41: New exercises every week

One of the hardest parts of being a personal trainer is keeping variety in the workouts. You can become stale by only showing your clients the same exercises. This will also eventually decrease your clientele. What I do is have an exercise of the week for every week so I am constantly showing new exercises and new techniques to everyone throughout the year. This keeps work outs fresh and enjoyable. The clients will look forward to learning new exercises. I have a dry erase board and I watch members walking in and look forward to seeing what the "Exercise of the Day" is.

Rule 42: Go to Different Fitness Events

Experience what an athlete must go through in a contest or competition format. If you are going to be a personal trainer and you have a client who would like to become a body builder, but you have no idea what to do, refer that client to a personal trainer who has had experience in body building.
Then go to see a body building contest. This will give you a better perspective of what body building is all about. Go to see a power lifting meets go to an Olympic weightlifting contest. This will make you a great Personal Trainer. The iron sports started with Body Building, Olympic weightlifting and Powerlifting. If you don't know these grass roots lifts, you should get to know them now.

Rule 43: Get Involved

To become successful, you must be in the eye of the community. Don't act like a hermit crab. Get involved in your neighborhood's activities. Go to neighborhood health fairs, your neighborhood town watch, coach one of the town's midget soccer teams, or even run for a political position such as mayor of your town. The more of a figurehead you are, the better business will be. People love to be near people who are successful and are good members of their community. This also holds true outside of your community. Get involved in coaching or judging Olympic weightlifting meets, body building contests or Powerlifting meets.

Rule 44: Join organizations

Joining both trade and community organizations can be very beneficial. Trade organizations gets your name out in your field and community organizations gets your name out to people in your area. The organization's and fellow member's websites and social networking now may include you and your company. This can spider web to other people's websites and organizations which in turn will give you more exposure.

Rule 45: Reward Your Clients

If your clients achieve a certain goal, you may want to reward them with a tee shirt. If they have lost a certain amount of weight, give them a gift. If they have attended 50 consecutive workout sessions they should also receive a gift.
Remember, people love to receive gifts, especially when they are free! They mean something to each member. Members like to talk about their trainers and about their accomplishment and the rewards they receive. It can be as little as a certificate. One of my promotions is "Your Goals are Our Goals". If they reach their

goals they get a certificate and 10% off their next personal training session.

Rule 46: Do Not be Cheap when Considering Client Gifts

Many personal trainers will give a gift for being involved in their organization or as advertising. Keep in mind this is
your image. Don't be cheap! This gift will reflect on your business. If you are going to give a gift make sure it is some- thing you would like. Be professional. This is one time where it's not the thought that counts. If the recipient does not appreciate the item, you have defeated your own purpose. Remember, the gift is a reflection of you and your business. I have a special, complete 48 sessions by a certain date and receive a free gym bag.

Rule 47: Brand yourself

Large companies do it, small companies do it, why shouldn't you? Find something that makes YOU and advertise it to all. For example, in all of my Facebook messages, I end with this statement "You are #1". To go further, I had a custom made earring done that shows "#1". All of this ties into my image, which is my brand, which people will remember.

Rule 48: Develop a Newsletter to Talk Up Your Service, Your Clients and You

This will increase your business. I have a free newsletter service that I provide to my clients every two months. This has been very effective for me. It allows me to talk to my clients and give out new and current information on health and fitness.

This also allows me to communicate on a personal level with my clients, for example, congratulating clients on their birthdays, weightlifting achievements and general fitness knowledge.

Rule 49: E-mail

Secure an e-mail account. This will allow you to communicate with your clients during the course of their busy day. **My email address is steve@tazunmi.com. I would love to hear from you!**

Rule 50: Webpage

Investigate getting a website. This will provide you with a company identity, and the ability to advertise and sell your products and services on-line. It has been and invaluable tool for me.

Rule 51: Use PayPal or other means to use Credit Cards

Give your members more options when it is time to pay. With the incorporation of Paypal, I have made it easier for my clients to pay me.

Rule 52: Plan social events

Even though personal training is a one on one relationship, having social events allow clients to meet other clients and to socialize. For example, twice a year I have an Hibachi Dinner for my clients. This enhances their experience and they tell more people about my service. Another great idea was an International Day. Everyone brings a dish that depicts their heritage. Then they talked alittle bit about it. It was very successful and boy was it fun.

Rule 53: Facebook, Twitter and other Social Networking Sites

Social networking sites can be a very useful tool with trying to get your message out to the public. Hundreds of millions of people go on these sites everyday. I personally use Facebook. I have a fanpage that I use to increase the amount of people who know about my service. I have gotten clients from this. Other sources are Twitter and LinkedIn, among many others.

Rule 54: Youtube

This is an excellent place to showcase the successes of your clients. Not only do your clients enjoy seeing their accomplishments, it shows the world what is possible with your help. I have noticed that members enjoy seeing other members on Youtube.

Rule 55: Utilize Ebay, Craigslist and Yardsales

Even though it may be used, if it is in good working condition and nothing is wrong with it, a piece of equipment that is used is still a new to your clients. A good source to buy equipment is Ebay, Craigslist and yardsales. You can find good pieces of equipment for a lot less then if you went to a retailer.

Rule 56: Give to People Who Have Less than You

Donate your time to the needy. Donate your money to your favorite cause. You are only on this earth a very short time. You will be remembered not by how many clients you had, or by being a trainer to a star. Your memory will be respected if you lived as a good, caring human being who gave a part of themselves to the needy or to a good cause. Make this earth a better place to live. You don't only have to give during the holidays. There are 365 days in which you can contribute according to your ability.

Rule 57: Have a cancellation policy

This could be a double edged sword. If you charge someone they may accept it, but you may never see them as a client again. On the other hand, if you don't charge them they may continue to cancel with no notice because there is no consequence. My policy is with a 24 hour notice there is no charge, less than 24 hour notice a $15.00 charge.

Rule 58: Use Barter

Bartering has been a form of payment since the beginning of civilization. This can be a very useful tool. However, you must make sure both parties are in agreement about the terms. Make sure it is well defined. What you never want to do is to not fulfill your obligation for a session or sessions. The session must be of the same high quality as any session paid for the conventional way.

NOTE: If a client has prepaid for sessions prior to the barter, you should do the barter sessions first then go back to the paid sessions.

Rule 59: Use Your Cell Phone Appropriately

In today's society, the cell phone is used throughout the entire day. With the invention of the smartphone you can photograph and video sessions to track progress.

If you accept a call during a session it takes away from your client's time and can be detrimental to your business. You can keep your phone with you so that you can use its features but put the ringer on vibrate and let calls go to voicemail during the session. DO NOT answer your phone during a session. Keep in mind, this is your members time, not yours.

Rule 60: Client's Cell Phones

Clients may also bring in their smartphone to video and record their progress. This is an excellent feature for them to show their friends what they are accomplishing with you and this is free advertising. However, they may take calls while they are working out because of work or socialization. Although you cannot forbid it, it is not something you should encourage because it will disrupt the flow of the workout. When I personally lift, I keep my phone off or not in the gym so I have 100% concentration on my lifting.

Rule 61: Don't get hung up on location

I hear it all the time in real estate, Location, Location, Location is the key for a successful business. I totally disagree. It has nothing to do with location. It is your talent, your certifications, your interactions with your clients and your personality that makes you a very successful personal trainer. For example, I live in a very rural area that is about 35 minutes from Philadelphia, PA. I have a person that travels two and half hours to see me once a week from Maryland. Most of my clients travel between 10 and 40 minutes to my location. A client will travel far distances for great service.

Rule 62: Take pictures of your clients

In my upstairs gym I have pictures of past and present clients. The clients like it and perspective clients are impressed. These pictures are also on my website, **www.tazunmi.com**.

Rule 63: Hall of Fame Pictures

In your office you should designate an area that is for your elite success stories. This is a great place to put your before and after pictures, testimonials, champions and record breakers.

Rule 64: You Should Never Be Under the Influence of Any Alcohol or Drugs During Any Workout Sessions

This will definitely destroy your business and you don't need me to explain why!

Rule 65: Practice What You Preach

I define service as servicing not only your clients, but also yourself. Because you are the product that a client is buying, if you are not 100 percent, you cannot give 100 percent.

You must work out. You must show the world that you are in shape. You are selling yourself and you are demonstrating the result of fitness and that requires being in great shape! Remember Jack LaLane. At the age of 90 he looked great! You are a walking billboard. If you look great it will increase your income.

Rule 66: Take 4 Vacations A Year

Your frame of mind is very important. As a personal trainer, you must fill many roles. You are a friend, you are a coach, you are a trainer, you are a therapist, you are a teacher. Your client is not the only one getting a workout. Because of this, the burn-out rate is very high. A doctor once told me that a person should take four vacations a year. They don't have to be long vacations, but I do mean that you should take four vacations a year. A vacation for you could be a long weekend without your children and spouse. The vacations should be taken throughout the four seasons. This will make you sharp and a better trainer and is absolutely necessary if you want to stay on top of your field.

Enjoy your life, it is too short. I have seen so many people save their money for their entire life so they could enjoy their retirement and to go on a long-awaited vacation only to find out that they are not physically or mentally able to enjoy their retirement. So take your vacations and enjoy every minute you are on this planet. See the world. Treat yourself every single day. YOU are #1 and YOU deserve it!

Rule 67: The Most Important Rule of All - Have Fun

Enjoy working with your clients, enjoy being with your family, enjoy being with your children, enjoy being with your friends. Have fun. Laugh and play. When was the last time you laughed out loud? Have a sense of humor. Laugh and be merry. This is what it is all about-enjoying your job, and having fun with it. It takes 43 muscles to frown and 17 to smile, so in other words, be happy and smile.

In Closing...

Our Family
Bozley, Kenji, Heather, Steven and Rose

There are a few points I would like to make in reference to starting your own personal training business. I feel that that today's world is changing so fast that some of the information I give you today may be obsolete tomorrow. There are three subjects I would like to briefly touch on. I felt that these subjects did not need an entire chapter but are definitely worth mentioning.

I am alarmed at what I see out there in the fitness world. If you are smart or can take a written test well, you can pass a written test of 300 to 400 questions and you are now considered a personal trainer, with no hands-on experience. **This scares me to death!** There are so many certifications out there, you really have to investigate to see what is good and what isn't. Make sure your certification includes hands- on experience, not only theory. A weekend course does not make you a personal trainer. If you are not fully qualified as a personal trainer, you can cause a client harm, or worse.

Check references before spending your money. Talk to other personal trainers - talk to teachers in the fitness field. I am not saying all certifications are bad, I am just recommending that you investigate and ask a lot of questions before enrolling in any certification program.

'There are many certifications that are credible and very good. Keep in mind the fitness world is always changing!

The next topic I would like to talk about is insurance. This is a new world-people are lawsuit happy! People are suing over hot coffee spilling on them. You must have insurance.
If you are training someone without insurance today I will tell you that you are **crazy!** Don't think Mr. Happy Jones will not sue you if he gets injured. Mr. Happy Jones can make your life miserable. When I started in this business 25 years ago, I had a very hard time

getting insurance. Today, there are many types of personal training insurance: gym insurance, aerobic insurance etc. I suggest you discuss your coverage with your insurance agent, or check the fitness magazines for advertisements or articles about add-on insurance. This is what I did to get my insurance. The insurance industry is always changing!

Let's discuss agreements and contracts. If you make up your own agreement or contract you should consult your attorney. If you make your agreement too restrictive your client will be dissatisfied and can negatively affect your business. For example, let's say you have a clause in your agreement which states "if a client is 15 minutes late, or fails to appear, the client will be charged for the session. Due to a family emergency your client doesn't make a session. When they come in for the next session they find they are being charged for the missed session. Your member will most likely search for another trainer who is more flexible. Again, check with your attorney. You'll have to live with this agreement and so do your clients. Laws, agreements and contracts are always changing

My wish for every one reading this book is that you become very successful! I hope this book will help you achieve your goal in life! This book is not only for Personal Training, the lessons in this book can be applied to any business and life situations, so tell a friend. Thank you for taking the time to read this book.

If there is any thing I can do to help you, please write me a letter or give me a call. I would love to hear your feedback, positive or negative, of the book. I would also love to hear from all of you on your successes. You can reach me at: **Steven Kenji Tazumi, Tazunmi Personal Training Service, PO Box 246, Mullica Hills NJ 08062, e-mail: steve@tazunmi.com. www.tazunmi.com**

Lastly, I would like to offer the following thanks:

...to Rose Carbonell, my significant other, who has helped in the second addition of this book. Without Rose's support I would have never accomplished this goal.

...to Kenji and Heather for letting daddy work on this book and Bozley, my dog, for not chewing up this book.

...special thanks to three members of my family who have changed my entire life: my loving mother and father Terrie and Tats Tazumi and my guardian angel, Uncle Tosh Oye.

...to my sister Lisa Tazumi for all of her help.

...to Tom and Nikki Patterson for all of their support.

...to Joshua Konstantinos for his original design of our webpage.

...to Joseph Invidiata for his endless hours on the phone helping me with this book.

...to Allen Louie for his timeless hours helping me to compose this book on my computer.

...to Dave Popivchak the best sales trainer I know.

...to John and Colleen Masciarelli for being great friends, and always being there.

...to Diane Wolbrecht for all of her technical knowledge and help.

...to all of my friends and associates.

. . .and last, but definitely not least, I would like to thank you for reading this book. I wish you much success!

Domo Arigato (Japanese) Thank you very much

Have a Great Day!

Remember:
You Are

#1

Don't You Ever Forget It!

Notes:

Notes:

Notes:

Notes:

_____

_____

_____

_____

_____

_____

_____

_____

_____

_____

_____

_____

_____